THIS BOOK is to
commemorate the issuance of the
Wichita medal
July 15, 1976
and is limited to 15,000 copies
No. 10225

WICHITA GRASSHOUSE, located in the Wichita Tribal Park, constructed by participants in the Wichita Cultural Program. This type of dwelling was what the Wichita people inhabited when Coronado first visited in 1541.

THE
PEOPLE
CALLED
WICHITA

by W.W. Newcomb, Jr.

Scientific Editor: Henry F. Dobyns
General Editor: John I. Griffin

PUBLISHED BY INDIAN TRIBAL SERIES / PHOENIX

NEWTON LAMAR
President, Wichita Tribe

M r. Newton Lamar was born near Gracemont, Oklahoma. As was the custom, he was reared by his full-blood Wichita Indian grandparents, so he is able to speak the Wichita language fluently. He is also cognizant of the traditions and customs of his tribe. He attended the Riverside Indian School until his enlistment in the Air Force in September, 1946. He served until February, 1952, at which time he was a Staff Sergeant with the Strategic Air Command. After his discharge, he was a student at Oklahoma A & M Technical College, Okmulgee, Oklahoma, and later attended the University of Wyoming and the University of Oklahoma.

Mr. Lamar was in the field of Law Enforcement from April, 1956 to January, 1965, and worked in Montana, Wyoming and New Mexico. In February, 1965, he accepted a position with the Public Relations Department, Navajo Tribe, Window Rock, Arizona. This experience proved valuable and afforded him many opportunities. His goal had always been to return to Oklahoma where he could work with and for his people, the Wichitas, whom he felt had been overlooked and almost forgotten by the federal government and other agencies. In January, 1971, he moved to Anadarko, Oklahoma, with his wife, Catherine, son Walter, and three daughters, Marsha, Regina and Judith. Since then, his time and efforts have been devoted to tribal business. He became Vice-President of the Wichita Tribe in 1972 and President in 1974. He was re-elected as President in July, 1976 for a four year term. During his tenure as a tribal official, he has worked toward restoring pride to the proud, but humble, Wichita people.

Other than his role as President of the Wichita Tribe, Mr. Lamar is employed as the Executive Director of the WCD Enterprises, Inc. The latter was formulated by the Wichita, Caddo, and Delaware Tribes for economic development purposes. In addition to the above-mentioned offices, he is a Commissioner on the Caddo Housing Authority; Member of the Board of Directors for ASCOG, a State Planning District; serves on the Executive Board of the Oklahoma Area Health Advisory Board which is comprised of thirty-six tribes; Vice-Chairman of the United Tribes of western Oklahoma and Kansas involving twenty-three tribes and a member of the National Indian Litigation Committee sponsored by the National Congress of American Indians.

Photograph by Settle Studio of Photography
NEWTON LAMAR, President of the Wichita Indian Nation.

In the old days, their name for themselves was *Kitikiti'sh* or *Kirikirish*, perhaps meaning "pre-eminent men" or "paramount among men." It is an old word, dating to another, almost forgotten time when the world, their world, was very different. Then, the *Kitikiti'sh* lived in the heartland of North America in the fertile valleys of the south-central plains in what is now Kansas and Oklahoma. They had been there so long that memory of where they had come from was hazy. They belonged to that land, and it to them, for there were few who challenged them. They were, indeed, pre-eminent men.

They were a gardening and hunting people who lived in grass lodge villages throughout the spring and summer while the women cultivated large, productive gardens of corn, beans, squash and tobacco. After the harvest was safely stored in the fall, they all but abandoned their scattered villages and became a roving, hunting people, living in tipis while the men pursued the great herds of bison that swarmed over

1

the plains. In the spring they returned to their villages to plant gardens. They also hunted deer, bear, antelope, and they made good use of the wild plums, grapes, and other fruits and plant foods that grew in their rich land. Like many other Plains Indians, they did not regard fish as edible.

It was a successful way to live in the plains country that suffers fierce, periodic droughts. During the dry times when the crops burned up, they depended more heavily on game. When game could not be found — particularly the bison, whose movements were erratic and unpredictable — they did not go hungry, because they could rely on their garden produce. They were also provident people who smoked or sun dried surplus meat and dried excess garden produce to store in hide bags and in underground cache pits. It is said that cache pits were so well constructed and concealed that when they had to flee their homes during the Civil War, the dried corn stored in cache pits was still edible when they returned some five years later. They were ingenious in preserving food, too. Pumpkins, for example, were cut into long, narrow strips, flattened by pounding, and when dried were woven into easily stored and transported mats. In later years, these mats became an important article of trade with tribes that did not plant.

The *Kitikiti'sh*, ancestors of the modern Wichitas, were not a nation or even a homogeneous people. Instead, there were six, seven, or perhaps more major subdivisions or sub-tribes, each of which was

2

made up of a number of essentially independent villages. Most of the subdivisions spoke one or the other dialect of Wichita, a Caddoan language, but the Kichais, although like the Wichitas in other ways, spoke a different Caddoan language. Only rough estimates can be made of their total population, but they appear to have numbered between 38,000 and 50,000 people when first known to Europeans.

There were other peoples in the plains who spoke Caddoan languages and lived much like the Wichitas. They were the Pawnees to the north and west in Nebraska, and the Arikaras farther north in the Dakotas. To the southeast, in southeastern Oklahoma, parts of Arkansas, Louisiana, and east Texas were more than two dozen Caddo tribes, joined together in several confederacies, pursuing a different kind of life from the Caddoan-speaking peoples in the plains, only their tongue signaling an ancient affinity.

In the old days the unfortified villages of the Wichitas, counting a thousand and more lodges, were often clustered together, like beads on a string, along ridges and terraces overlooking particularly attractive and productive river bottom lands. Their round grass houses were substantial, comfortable dwellings. They varied from fifteen to thirty feet in diameter, accommodating in the average lodge ten to twelve people. They were constructed on a framework of upright forked posts, joined by posts laid in their crotches. Long, slender poles were laid against

3

A WICHITA SETTLEMENT IN 1834. George Catlin, famed painter of North American Indians visited. From *Letters and Notes on the Manners, Customs, and Conditions of the North American*

accompanied a United States Dragoon expedition and drew the "Pawnee Pict" village it
Indians. Vol. II, Plate 173, 1841.

these, and their upper ends tied together. Other, lighter poles were tied horizontally to these, and coarse grass was spread over the exterior from the ground up. More poles were added to secure the grass covering against the prairie wind.

Each house had two low, narrow doorways, one on the east, the other on the west. The doors themselves being of grass tied to a willow framework. Beds were arranged around the interior walls, constructed of light poles and raised well above the floor. Hide curtains decorated with paintings hung around the beds, covered with bison-hides, afforded some privacy. A slight excavation was made in the center of the dwelling for a fire, and a small vent for smoke was provided near the top of the roof. Near the grass houses were open-sided arbors, constructed like the houses, but somewhat larger with an oval floorplan and equipped with raised floors. There the family rested and worked during the summer heat. Other arbors, from ten to twenty feet square, were used to dry and store meat, corn, and other crops. Unmarried, carefully-guarded girls slept in thatched huts built on platforms.

A chief, who was accorded a good deal of respect, governed each village with a sub-chief and a number of lesser officials. Although villages were politically independent, many kinship and social ties linked nearby villages, so eminent chiefs, particularly of large villages, were apt to exert considerable authority over lesser ones. Men became chiefs by being elected by an informal council of outstanding war-

6

WETARASHARO, an elderly Wichita chief who dealt with United States Dragoon officers in 1834, sketched by artist George Catlin, showing the dignified mein, and symbols of leadership status worn by a tribal chief. From *Letters and Notes on the Manners, Customs, and Conditions of the North American Indians.* Vol. II, Plate 174, 1841.

riors, and any man, through his wisdom or exploits, might attain the office. The council of warriors curbed any autocratic tendencies a chief might show, and it appears that chiefs were mainly concerned with foreign affairs.

There was little need for a formal governmental structure to regulate and control the internal affairs of the villages, for these matters were handled primarily by the matriarchal families. A woman, her husband, unmarried children, daughters and their husbands with their children composed these basic social and economic units. Such a family might occupy one lodge, or perhaps several close together if the family were large, and the oldest woman of such households was its head and supervisor. Other related families appear to have built their dwellings nearby, perhaps accounting for the clusters of houses noted by early European explorers. The women of the households cooperatively tilled fields, gathered firewood, tanned hides, sewed clothing, prepared food, and built houses. The men helped in the physically more demanding tasks of house-building, but generally their occupations were those of hunter and warrior. During the hunting season, the households were broken up, but they maintained cohesiveness by pitching their tipis close to one another.

When the birth of a child was at hand, an expectant woman moved out of her grass lodge to a tipi pitched nearby. Birth was regarded as supernaturally dangerous, and husbands were barred from entering the tipi until four days after the infant's birth, lest

8

they cause mother and child to become ill. Expectant women were attended by experienced, elderly midwives, and shortly after birth another older woman, who was knowledgeable about one of the important deities, Bright Shining Woman, took the infant to a river and bathed it, while praying to her and to another important deity, Man-Never-Known-On-Earth, for the welfare of the child.

Children were quickly immersed in the intimate, close-knit world of the matriarchal family. Unlike the modern American custom in which single terms are used for each close (and important) relative (such as "father," "sister"), the Wichita family was one in which a number of different and more distant, collateral relatives were grouped together under such terms. The result was that a large body of relatives was brought into a close and intimate working relationship. A Wichita child, for example, used the terms "brother" and "sister," and the appropriate behavior, to include all of his cousins. The child lived in the same household with the children of his maternal aunt (his mother's sister), and, in fact, because men sometimes married sisters, she also might be married to the child's father.

Following this kind of pattern and logic, a person termed his mother's sisters, "mother," qualifying the term with "little" or "big" depending upon whether they were younger or older than the mother. Similarly, a father's brothers were "little" or "big" fathers. Inasmuch as the Wichitas practiced the levirate, a custom in which a man married his brother's widow, the brothers of a child's father were potential fathers. A father's sister was also termed and treated like a big or little mother, but a mother's brother was termed uncle, indicating the maternal orientation of their families. In the grandparental generation all relatives were referred to as grandfather or grandmother, with the qualifying "big" or "little" depending upon the relative age of the connecting grandparent. Reciprocally, all grandchildren and the grandchildren of a person's siblings were termed grandchildren.

As children grew, fathers played an increasingly important role in the instruction of their sons in hunting, the use of weapons, and the other manly arts. Mothers and the other women of the household trained girls in the many activities of their sex. Girls approaching marriageable age were kept away from men and boys. The families of marriageable boys usually arranged, through go-betweens, marriage with the family of the chosen girl, ideally a gift of the same village. Marriages were formalized by giving presents to and a feast for the bride's relatives.

The newly married couple lived in the household of the bride's parents, and the new son-in-law was expected to perform a number of duties for the family, the most important being to supply them with meat. His standing with the family depended upon how well he fulfilled this and other obligations. The relationships between in-laws, particularly those of the opposite sex, were always reserved and formal. Thus, a man's mother-in-law might talk to

10

him through his wife rather than directly to him, and a man would never tease or joke with a mother-in-law no matter how successful or prestigious he might become.

The unfortified villages with dispersed lodges suggest that before the European invasion the Wichita people were essentially peaceful. After the advent of Europeans, bitter competition developed between tribes for firearms, horses, and European goods. Intertribal strife and Wichita involvement in it increased tremendously. The Wichita pattern of warfare, with small raiding parties composed of volunteers who counted coup on their enemies and bragged of their exploits on long winter nights before their peers, was typically in the Plains tradition. In the eighteenth century the Wichitas marshaled what amounted to armies and fought sustained battles. They had become a warrior people, and the most honored men were successful warriors.

When a person was on the verge of death, relatives began to gather around, and all relatives were expected to be present when the body was buried. Non-relatives took charge of the last rites, however, because the souls of the dead were believed to attempt to persuade relatives to join them. Relatives cut their hair in mourning, close relatives cutting off more hair than distant ones. Burial generally occurred two to four days after death. Burial was in a shallow grave with the head oriented to the east, in cemeteries located on hills near the villages. Non-relatives came to mourn with the bereaved relatives who gave them

11

presents. The family of the deceased often impoverished itself through such give-aways. Relatives mourned for four days and surviving spouses for several months.

The Wichitas believed in a pantheon of gods and goddesses, arranged in a vaguely-graded hierarchy, and divided into sky and earth, male and female deities. Chief among them was *Kinnikasus*, creator of the universe and all within it. The sun, Man-Reflecting-Light, was sometimes associated and merged with him, sometimes distinguished. Morning Star, spirit of the first man, ushered in the daylight, ruled the other stars, and stood next in the hierarchy, followed by a number of other celestial gods. Among them was North Star, from whom shamans acquired their powers. The most important female celestial being was Bright Shining Woman, the moon goddess, who was the wife of Morning Star, and the first woman created. She was particularly important to women for she controlled the forces of reproduction and procreation of humans, animals, and crops. Almost as important as Bright Shining Woman and associated with her was a water goddess, Woman-Forever-In-The-Water. She provided water for drinking, rain for crops, and was responsible for the cleansing and healing properties of water. She was also a guardian of feminine virtue, helping a woman remain chaste while her husband was away on the hunt or warpath. Another terrestrial goddess, Earth Mother, was held to have given birth to everything; she nourished and preserved man and

12

supplied the herbs and other medicines used to cure the ill. She was also associated with the wind, and consequently with the breath, and so with life and death. Those who were about to embark on a journey always directed a prayer to her.

In addition to the major deities, every sort of animate and inanimate object might contain or possess more than natural qualities. Animals often assumed special supernatural power and appeared to men in dreams or in revelations to become their lifelong guardian spirits. All spiritual knowledge was believed to come from such experiences. Yet neither boys nor men actively sought guardian spirits by fasting, or self-torture in isolated places, as was practiced by some Plains tribes. Wichitas believed in a continuing existence in a spirit world after death, denied only to those who had taken their own lives.

The gods and goddesses who controlled or were responsible for the general or tribal welfare were propitiated by semi-secret religious societies. How many of these there were in the old days is unknown, but in the early years of the twentieth century fourteen dance societies, including three that were women's societies, were still remembered. Membership in these societies was open to anybody who wished to join. The deer dance, a ceremony conducted by societies of medicine men or shamans, was held in the spring when the green grass first appeared, then when the corn was ripening, and finally when the corn was harvested. Its general purpose was to purge evil influences and promote health, longevity, and prosperity. One of the more popular dances, performed by a secret society, was known as the Calumet Pipe Sticks. It was sanctioned by one of the old myths, and its performance was thought to be of lasting benefit to the tribe. Performances of other societies insured successful harvests, the propagation of bison, and the good fortune of war parties.

Children learned about the supernatural world from an elderly man who was especially invited by a family to come into its lodge and instruct them. He was a respected elder, a man who had been brave, kind, modest, and decent throughout his life. His recitation of the tribal lore was in itself a form of prayer, dividing the tales into four parts, according to the four eras of Wichita cosmology. The first era concerned with the creation of the world and the first man and woman, who became Morning Star and Bright Shining Woman, after their tasks on earth were completed. The second era was one of transformation; people learned again of their power, scattered over the earth, named themselves, and turned into animals whose names they had taken. It was also a time of wrongdoing by people, animals, and celestial beings, and ultimately a deluge was sent to destroy the world. But two people survived the flood to inaugurate the third and modern era. The couple was given an ear of corn and bows and arrows and taught the various skills and knowledge that Wichitas possessed. The couple taught their children about the ancient world, and their children followed their instructions. Consequently, they were given power

14

by the animals and were taught their secrets. The children also learned they were mortal, as one person who had died returned from the spirit world to give them their knowledge of life after death.

The fourth era of decline and disaster was close at hand. The earth would no longer produce the things people needed, and they would no longer be able to accomplish anything. Weeds would grow in the place of corn; animals, trees, and even running water would talk to man; incest would take place; no babies would be born. Men would lose their reason and judgment, and ultimately the world would become uninhabitable. At the end an eminent man would be selected by a star to explain to the people what was happening. Then the stars and the sun would become human again, as in the early days, and the cycle of creation, transformation, decline, disintegration, and rebirth would begin again.

In a way, as these pages will relate, one might regard much of the Wichita experience during the past 400 years to be a fulfillment of the fourth era prophecy. So viewed, the wheel has turned, an era of regeneration and creation is at hand.

COMING OF THE SPANIARDS

In the summer of 1541, Don Francisco Vásquez de Coronado, with thirty picked men, rode into a peaceful farming village in the heart of North America. It was the first meeting between Spaniards and the people of Quivira, a people known today as Wichitas.

15

A year before, Coronado had led an army of more than 1,000 well-equipped men northward out of Mexico in search of the fabled seven golden cities of Cibola. They turned out to be the adobe villages in New Mexico of the Pueblo Indians known today as Zuñis. Thwarted by the absence of the expected wealth at Zuñi, and elsewhere in the puebloan country, Coronado and his conquistadores spent the winter at pueblos near the Rio Grande. By spring they were impatient to seek their fortunes in another land. They had heard of a wealthy kingdom, the land of Quivira, where there were said to be great cities of stone houses, where the people used gold vessels, and possessed other riches. So Coronado's army rode eastward into the flat bison country of the southern plains that summer. The Spaniards had been fooled, however, or perhaps their greed led them to hear what they wanted most to hear. For the great cities turned out to be villages of grass houses, and the only metal they found was a piece of copper a chief wore as a necklace and some copper bells. There was no gold or silver. The wealth of this land was of another kind: it lay on its fertile soil, in the innumerable herds of bison that often blackened it, and in its people who had long since learned to live abundantly on its riches.

Coronado's Quivira lay within the great bend of the Arkansas River, in what is now south-central Kansas. He spent almost a month there, traveling about sixty-five miles through Wichita villages, and he probably did not visit all of them. These people

16

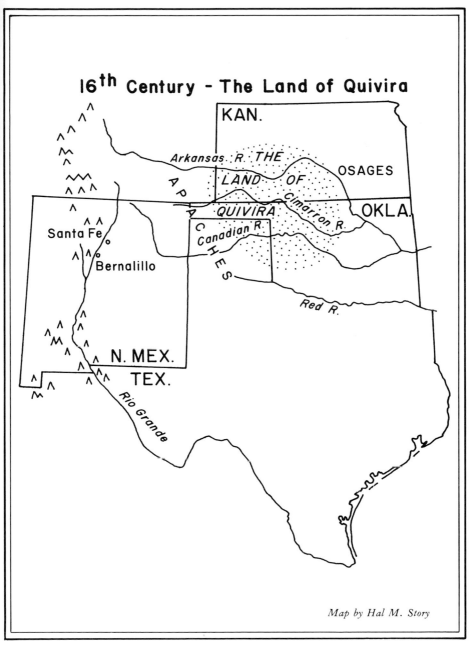

16th Century - The Land of Quivira

KAN.

Arkansas R. THE

LAND OF

OSAGES

QUIVIRA

Cimarron R.

OKLA.

APACHES

Canadian R.

Santa Fe

Bernalillo

Red R.

N. MEX.

TEX.

Rio Grande

Map by Hal M. Story

MAP 1.

were not newcomers; their ancestors had lived in this land for at least five centuries. Traces of their houses and other buildings, the outlines of the cache pits they dug, and the other more or less indestructable rubble of their lives have been discovered in archeological sites extending from central Kansas southward through Oklahoma.

Remembrance of Coronado's mounted men must have been fast fading by the time Spanish foreigners again rode into the lands of the Wichitas. For it was more than a half century later that Francisco Leyva de Bonilla and Antonio Gutiérrez de Humaña led an unauthorized expedition from New Mexico to Quivira. They reached a large Wichita village on the Arkansas River in eastern Kansas, then continued on. Several days after leaving the village, Humaña murdered Bonilla, then, a week later on the banks of a large river, the Indian guides deserted. Finally, Humaña and most of the remaining members of the party were killed by Indians. One of the guides, named Jusephe, eventually returned to New Mexico where he was questioned by the Spaniards. He could recount but little of the expedition and the people they had met.

A few years later, in 1601, Don Juan de Oñate, the colonizer of New Mexico, led an expedition into the same region. He had listened to Jusephe's story and had dreams of exploring Quivira and the lands beyond. He set out in June with more than seventy picked men, two friars, more than 700 horses and mules, as well as carts, four cannons, and servants to

18

carry the baggage. After leaving the mountains, the expedition followed the valley of the Canadian River eastward, soon meeting friendly bison-hunting Apaches. Encountering sand dunes, probably the Antelope Hills just east of the Texas Panhandle, the expedition turned to the northeast, traveling easily through flat and verdant country. Before reaching the Wichita villages the explorers encountered a large encampment of Escanjaques, a people who were enemies of the Wichitas and only too happy to guide the Spaniards, assuming they had come to avenge the slaying of Humaña. In spite of his guides, Oñate was able to meet the Wichita in peace. The Wichitas greeted the Spaniards by throwing some of the beads they wore among the strangers, then invited them into their lodges, and brought them ears of corn and large round loaves of cornmeal bread.

The next day, however, when Oñate learned that the Wichitas were responsible for the death of Humaña and others of his party, he had a prominent chief, Catarax, seized and put into irons. Catarax coolly signaled his people to withdraw, which they did, abandoning their village on the opposite bank of the river. Oñate forded the stream and occupied the village of some 1,200 houses. He was amazed at the neatly constructed, round houses of poles and grass thatching. Much corn had been harvested and left behind in the village, and another crop of corn was already up in the fields surrounding the village.

The following day Oñate and his men left the village to continue their explorations. Finding the

19

country heavily populated, and realizing that the Wichitas were gathering their forces in order to overwhelm them, the Spaniards decided to withdraw. Catarax had already been freed, though still in shackles, by warriors who had feinted an attack on the Spaniards. The Wichitas permitted the Spaniards to withdraw with no further hostilities, but the Escanjaques did not. Perhaps angered that the Spaniards had not attacked the Wichitas, and surely irritated that the Spaniards had attempted to restrain them from looting the abandoned village, they fought a fierce battle with the Spaniards, before the Spaniards were able to turn homeward.

The lands of the Wichita were a long march from Santa Fe, and although Oñate had found many souls to save on the Arkansas, he estimated that it would take a force of 300 well-armed, mounted, and armored men to subdue these Indians first, and the land held few other attractions for the Spaniards. They did not come so far again, although seventeenth century Spanish expeditions probing the plains country continued to encounter Wichitas. In 1629, for example, Fray Juan de Salas and Fray Diego Lopez, while on the southern plains, were visited by a delegation of "Quivira" and "Aixaos" Indians who lived to the east, probably on the Canadian or Cimarron Rivers of northern Oklahoma. The Aixaos, like the Quiviras, were probably a Wichita subdivision, possibly the one known in later times as Taovayas. In 1684, Juan Dominguez de Mendoza led an expedition into west-central Texas, remaining there for several months killing bison and being visited by many groups of Indians. Among them were "Isconis," the Wichita Iscanis of later years.

Remote and isolated in the heart of the plains, the Wichita had only fleeting contacts with Spaniards. The consequences of the European invasion, nevertheless, began to affect the Wichita peoples before the seventeenth century had run its course. Horses and the knowledge of how to ride and care for them had soon spread from the Spanish settlements around Santa Fe to the native peoples. In the plains country, horses had a revolutionary impact, particularly among nomadic bison hunters, making a bison hunting life relatively easy and rewarding. Not only did the old bison hunters quickly adopt horses, but outsiders equipped with horses soon invaded the plains to also partake in this new kind of life.

For the Wichita peoples possession of horses might seem to have been less essential than for some, inasmuch as their womenfolk raised an abundance of corn, beans, and squash. Yet Wichita hunters were as eager to obtain these wonderful, serviceable animals as other plains people. Besides, soon it was essential that they do so, because mounted hunters were also mounted warriors. To hunt afoot one might only go hungry; to fight cavalry afoot was to court certain disaster.

COMING OF THE FRENCH TRADERS

Another consequence of the European presence was the spread of firearms to the native peoples.

21

While the Spaniards refused to supply Indians with firearms, French traders were quick to do so. Unfortunately for the Wichitas, the Osages, who lived to their north and east, acquired firearms from French traders before they were able to do so. Consequently, about the beginning of the eighteenth century, as a result of Osage military pressure from the north and east, and attacks by Comanches from the north and west, and possibly for other reasons, the Wichitas or at least the more northerly villages, began a southward migration and a consolidation of villages. By 1719, when visited by the Frenchman Claude-Charles Dutisné from Kaskaskia in the Illinois country, and Sieur Du Rivage and Bénard de la Harpe from Louisiana, Wichita villages were scattered from the vicinity of the Kansas-Oklahoma border south through the river valleys of eastern Oklahoma into Texas. The Wichita withdrawal to the south was to continue for another century, with villages eventually being established as far south as Waco, on the Brazos River in central Texas, the city taking its name from this sub-tribe.

By the time La Harpe and other Frenchmen opened trade with them, the Wichitas must have been well aware that their situation was precarious. The Osages, made militarily superior by their familiarity with and abundant supply of French firearms, could not be successfully repulsed until the Wichitas also acquired firearms and learned how to use them effectively. As the Wichitas moved southward, they invaded lands inhabited by Apaches, foes made for-

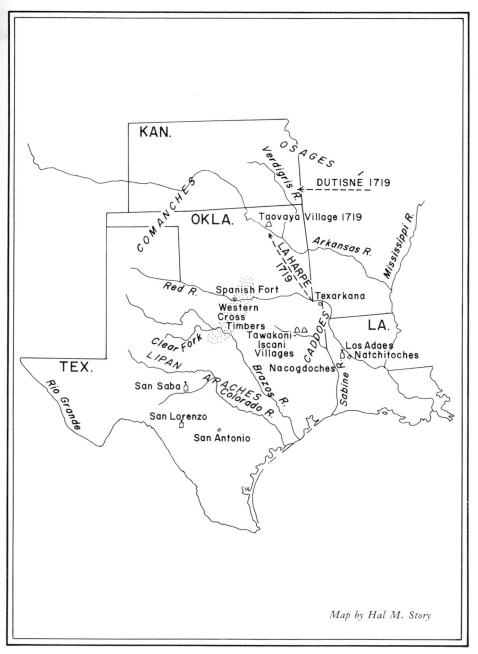

KAN.

OKLA.

TEX.

LA.

OSAGES

DUTISNÉ 1719

COMANCHES

Verdigris R.

Taovaya Village 1719

Arkansas R.

Mississippi R.

LA HARPE 1719

Red R.

Spanish Fort

Texarkana

Western
Cross
Timbers

Tawakoni
Iscani
Villages

CADDOES

Los Adaes
Natchitoches

Clear Fork

LIPAN

APACHES

Brazos R.

Nacogdoches

Sabine R.

San Saba

Colorado R.

Rio Grande

San Lorenzo

San Antonio

Map by Hal M. Story

MAP 2.

midable by their possession of a plentiful supply of horses. The Wichitas had also acquired some horses and learned the art of horsemanship before the opening of the eighteenth century, but horses were in relatively short supply and remained a precious commodity. The principle reason for this was the Comanches, who had invaded the southern plains about the beginning of the eighteenth century, cutting off the Wichitas from access to the Spanish settlements in New Mexico and their supply of horses. If the Wichitas were to survive under the conditions imposed directly and indirectly by the coming of Europeans, they had to secure firearms and a more adequate supply of horses. No wonder, then, that Bénard de la Harpe was greeted with much pomp and ceremony at a Tawakoni village in east-central Oklahoma in 1719.

In the spring of that year, La Harpe had established a trading post near modern Texarkana, just above the great bend of the Red River, in order to trade and make alliances with the Caddo Indians of that vicinity. He also was keenly interested in making contact and opening trade with the Spanish in New Mexico. La Harpe soon dispatched M. Du Rivage, with a few soldiers, some other Frenchmen of his party, and some Caddo warriors to make alliances with the upriver tribes. About one hundred miles upstream, Du Rivage encountered a mixed war party of Indians, including Quidehais (Kichai) and a number of other Indians, some of whom may also have been Wichita. They were returning from a

24

successful attack on an Apache camp situated some 150 miles up the Red River. To insure the friendship of the Kichais and the other Indians, Du Rivage distributed presents among them, then inquired about the peoples who lived to the north. He was told that the northern people were their allies, and that the principal nation was called "Touacara" (Tawakoni). Du Rivage suggested that La Harpe would like to visit these powerful people in order to form an alliance with them, but that he would need guides to lead him there. After conferring with one another, the leaders of the war party indicated that they would go to the Tawakoni village to inform them that the Frenchmen were coming, and they sent two Kichai guides back to the post on the Red River with Du Rivage.

France and Spain had gone to war again, so that it was useless for La Harpe to attempt to inaugurate trade with the Spanish in New Mexico. Exploration of the unknown country to the northwest and developing trade with its people was an attractive alternative. In August with the two Kichai guides and eight other men, La Harpe struck out on horseback for the Tawakoni village. The journey to the village, located on the Arkansas River above present Haskell, Oklahoma, took more than three weeks and was relatively uneventful, although they barely avoided a skirmish with a party of Osages and just managed to stay out of the way of an Apache war party.

La Harpe and his party were ceremoniously met some distance from the village by the principal chief of the Tawakonis and six chiefs of other "nations," all mounted on beautiful horses. Following a formal exchange of assurances of friendship, members of the French party were presented with cornmeal bread and dried meat, La Harpe was provided with a fine horse, and the group proceeded to the village. It seems to have been composed of at least two contiguous villages, set in a beautiful spot extending for several miles along a terrace overlooking the river. When the procession arrived at the village, the Indians had La Harpe dismount, a musket-shot away from the Tawakoni chief. A buffalo robe had been placed over a plank, and there he was seated. The leading men encircled him, and one after another put a hand in his as a gesture of goodwill. La Harpe presented the young Tawakoni chief with muskets, powder, balls, and cloth, and the chief gave La Harpe an eagle feather headdress, adorned with many colored feathers and two calumet feathers, one for peace and one for war. It was the most distinguished gift they could bestow.

The peoples who had gathered, in addition to the Tawakonis, were the Toayas (Tawehash or Taovaya, then the most populous Wichita subdivision), the Ousitas (Wichita proper, the subdivision whose name came to be employed for all of the subdivisions), and the Ascanis (Iscanis). The Caumuche, Aderos, Quataquois, Quicasquiris, and Honechas that La Harpe listed in his journal were almost surely Wichita subdivisions, too, but they cannot be positively identified with later Wichita subdivisions.

26

BESIDES GUNS, MUNITIONS, AND TEXTILES, French and later British and American traders supplied the Wichita people with jewelry of several types. This belle photographed by William S. Soule sports metal earrings, chains and pendants, and manufactured as well as Indian hand-made beads.

There was a good deal of protocol involved in dealing with foreigners, and in the next several days long, drawn-out calumet ceremonies were held for the French. Seven thousand persons had been attracted to the village to see the Frenchmen and to participate in the formalities. These were conducted by the Taovaya and Iscani chiefs, both of whom were old men skilled in leading such ceremonies. Speeches were made, dances held, the calumet smoked, and presents exchanged. The high point of the ceremonies occurred when La Harpe was carried to an arbor, and his face painted blue. Then he was presented with thirty buffalo robes, rock salt, tobacco pressed into loaves, some mineral pigments, and an eight-year-old Apache captive. The Taovaya chief apologized for having only one captive to give La Harpe, but the seventeen others they had possessed had been consumed in a public feast a month earlier. Cannibalism appears to have been engaged in for magical purposes, to gain the strength or bravery of their enemies by consuming them, not because of a ghoulish appetite for human flesh.

After receiving these gifts La Harpe reciprocated by giving the Wichitas the presents he had brought, and several days later left the village to return to his post on the Red River. He had planned on leaving some of his men behind at the village, pending approval of a trading post there, but he did not do so because the village would be abandoned in November by its residents for the winter hunt, from which they would not return until March. The return journey was hectic since the French no longer had the Kichai guides, food ran out, and the Caddo Indian who had accompanied them was killed by an Apache war party. Still La Harpe managed to reach the post on the Red River on October 13.

La Harpe left the first extensive account of how a Wichita people lived, and though some aspects of life had changed since they had been visited by Coronado almost 180 years earlier, life went on much as it had. The women were still raising bumper crops of corn, beans, squash, pumpkins, and tobacco in the rich bottom lands of the Arkansas valley. They made extensive use of the plums, mulberries, grapes, and other fruits and nuts that were found in abundance in this fertile country, and in addition to bison there was much game in the country. La Harpe learned that horses were highly prized by the Wichitas, and that they had come to depend upon them for the hunt and for war. They did not have as many horses as they wanted, and they protected them against enemy arrows and lances with leather breast plates. They were already raising some beautiful horses, and the saddles and bridles they manufactured in the Spanish style were well made.

The village chiefs were highly respected and shown much deference, and La Harpe found the men, in general, to be sensible and intelligent. To many it might seem that the Wichitas were leading an idyllic life. Yet La Harpe thought the men "slothful," because they habitually spent their time in the company of their chief, eating, smoking, and play-

29

ing games, at least when they were not preoccupied with affairs of the heart. La Harpe might have held a different opinion of the men had he had an opportunity to observe them on the hunt or at war. The women, he remarked, were handsome and tried to outdo one another in supplying the Frenchmen with tasty dishes and other things.

At almost the same time that La Harpe reached the Wichita villages on the Arkansas, another Frenchman, Claude-Charles Dutisné, was sent westward from the mouth of the Missouri River to contact the Wichitas. His purpose was to arrange alliances with the various tribes in order to open the way west to the Spaniards in New Mexico. He also hoped to discover silver or other mines as the Spanish were reported to have done, and more immediately, the French needed horses, and he hoped to find a plentiful supply in the west.

Dutisné first attempted to reach the Wichitas by boat, ascending the Missouri, but the Missouri Indians, living in a village in the vicinity of modern Miami, Missouri, would not permit him to pass, and he had to turn back. He again set out from Kaskaskia, this time traveling overland in July or August, 1719, heading directly westward by the compass. He was cordially received at an Osage village near the mouth of the Little Osage River in western Missouri, but like the Missouris, the Osages were dead set against Dutisné going to the Wichita country, inasmuch as he would open trade with them, and eventually they would acquire firearms. Dutisné

30

warned Osages that they would anger the French governor if they did not permit him to continue, implying that the French would break off trade with them. Dutisné added that he was determined to proceed and that he would take only three guns for himself and his interpreter. Although angry, the Osages allowed Dutisné to continue.

After four days travel Dutisné reached a village of people he referred to variously as "Panioussa," "Paneassa," and "Panis." This was the name used by the Osages and other Siouan-speaking peoples for the Wichita. It meant "black Pawnee" and perhaps referred to skin color, but more probably to the Wichita custom of heavily tatooing face, arms, and chest, a custom the more northerly Pawnees did not share. The French came to refer to the Wichitas as "Panis Piques," meaning tatooed or pricked Pawnees, and Americans, borrowing from them sometimes referred to Wichitas as "Pawnee Picts." Kiowas and Comanches also referred to them by names meaning tatooed faces, and their designation in the sign language is drawn from this custom.

The Wichita village Dutisné reached was apparently on the Verdigris River, near Neodesha in southeastern Kansas. The Wichitas did not give Dutisné a warm welcome, because the Osages had sent a runner ahead to warn them that he was coming to make slaves of them. Then Dutisné was able to convince the Wichitas that the Osages had lied about him, and they soon became more friendly and agreed to an alliance with the Frenchmen, no doubt because

31

they were eager to develop regular trade with them. The negotiations between the Wichitas and Dutisné were accompanied by as much pomp and ceremony as were those with La Harpe. Dutisné added that during the feasting, the hosts placed pieces of meat in the mouth of honored guests. Dutisné was unable to persuade the Wichitas to allow him to proceed on to the Apache villages which lay to the southwest. Like the Osages and Missouris, the Wichitas looked out for their own interests. The Wichitas were then involved in a bitter war with the Apaches "even eating each other," as La Harpe had also noted, and they did not want their enemies to acquire firearms.

The Wichita village Dutisné visited had 130 grass lodges and between 200-250 warriors. There was another village of the same size several miles upstream, and the two villages had about 300 horses between them. These animals were highly esteemed and the Wichitas did not wish to part with any of them; nevertheless, Dutisné was able to procure two horses and a mule with a Spanish brand for three muskets, powder, pickaxes, and some knives. If he had kept his promise to the Osages, the trade left him weaponless. For their part, the Wichitas had only six guns in the village, so that the acquisition of three more must have made the trade very worthwhile. Although they promised to bring more horses at Kaskaskia the next spring, they no longer were able to trade for them directly with the Spaniards, as Indian enemies — Apaches and Comanches —

32

KAH-KEE-TSE ("THE THIGHS") was a Wichita girl ransomed from the Osage Indians by a United States Dragoon expedition that returned her to her own people in 1834. George Catlin, the famous artist who accompanied the troops, sketched her in sufficient detail to record her tribal tatoos — the distinctive body tattooing that gave the Wichita their designation as the "Pawnee Picts."

blocked the way. The only souvenir of their former visits to Santa Fe was an old silver cup, which Dutisné acquired.

Dutisné did not gain much additional information about the Wichitas. He too learned that Wichita warriors used leather armor to protect their horses in war, and he said that the Wichitas were skillful fighters employing the bow and arrow and a long lance, tipped with the blade of a European sword. They told him that there were other Wichita villages off to the west and northwest, but oddly, they did not tell him of the villages on the Arkansas, scarcely one hundred miles to the southwest. La Harpe, on the other hand, had learned of the villages Dutisné visited.

By the mid-eighteenth century the two most prominent and now fortified Wichita villages adjoined each other on the Arkansas River, probably in what is now Kay County, in northern Oklahoma. For a time this was an ideal location, because in about 1747 the Comanches and Wichitas agreed to a mutually advantageous peace, thus making the Wichitas prosperous middlemen in the lucrative trade between the Comanches and the Frenchmen. French traders could ascend the Arkansas as far as the twin villages by boat, and the villages were easily accessible to the nomadic Comanches. In 1752, the Pawnees also made peace with the Comanches, and French traders took the more direct route from the Illinois country up the Missouri to the Pawnee

34

villages where they could trade or obtain horses for the journey to Santa Fe.

Before 1757, the villages on the Arkansas River had moved south to the Red River. There they were re-established just west of the Cross Timbers (a belt of timber and brush, extending in a north-south strip from Oklahoma into Texas). The Taovaya village on the north side of the river (in Jefferson County, Oklahoma) was fortified and an Iscani village was located a short distance downstream. By 1765, a Wichita (Wichita proper) village was located north of the Taovaya village and the Iscani village was south of the river. The Taovayas were numerically the strongest subdivision, and the Red River villages together counted more than 500 warriors. No doubt this represented a decrease over earlier years, but they still constituted a formidable force.

It was no accident that a superb location had been chosen for the Taovaya settlement. The second chief of each Wichita village was titled *okonitsa* ("one who locates"), one of his principal duties being to search out promising sites for settlement.

The new settlement on the Red River — misnamed "Spanish Fort" by Americans who settled at the abandoned site in the mid-nineteenth century — was an excellent choice. It bordered on the Comanche range to the west, could be reached by boat by traders from Natchitoches, Louisiana, and the Cross Timbers offered a plentiful source of timber for construction and fuel. There was a good ford, allow-

35

ing easy access to the other side of the river, a fine spring, plentiful arable land along the river, excellent pasturage for horses, and much bison and other game nearby. The only drawback to the new location was that it was within the old range of the Lipan Apaches, who soon raided the new settlement. The village was fortified to lessen this danger.

A Spanish soldier, Antonio Treviño, who was captured by the Taovayas in 1764, lived in the palisaded village for six months and left a description of it. Normally, adult males, and particularly Spanish soldiers, were killed when captured. Treviño had displayed such courage in battle, despite being severely wounded, that the Taovaya chief, Eyasaquiche, spared his life and nursed him back to health. He wanted Treviño to serve as an example to his own warriors and to help in their struggle against the Osages. Then the chief released Treviño in the interests of concluding peace with the Spaniards.

According to Treviño, and what is known about the site archeologically, the fortification consisted of an oval, log enclosure about 130 yards in its longest dimension, eighty-eight yards wide, and situated in the middle of their dispersed village on the banks of the river. It was constructed of split logs set vertically in the ground and spaced far enough apart so that muskets could be fired between them. Outside of the palisade was an earthen rampart about four feet high, and beyond it a ditch about four feet deep and more than twelve feet wide. Inside the palisade were four underground chambers large enough to shelter all

36

non-combatants of the village. In more peaceful days, before the onslaught of Europeans, the Wichitas had little or no need to build such ambitious fortifications. Once the Wichita became deeply involved in a desperate struggle with the Lipan Apaches and Osages, perhaps advised by the French, their fortress was to stand them in good stead.

CONFLICT WITH THE SPANIARDS

In 1757, the Spaniards had built a mission and presidio on the San Saba River in west-central Texas for the Lipan Apaches in an effort to end decades of bitter conflict with them. The missionaries could not persuade the Lipans to settle at the mission; however, they only stopped briefly on their way north to hunt and to make war, and on their return to the south. The Wichitas, Comanches, and other northern tribes, often referred to as *Norteños*, naturally concluded that the Spaniards and Apaches were fast friends. So in the spring of 1758, a combined force of Tonkawas, Tejas (Caddoes), Wichitas, Comanches, and other tribes, ostensibly hunting for Apaches, sacked and burned the mission, killing two of the missionaries and eight other people.

In the following year, Colonel Diego Ortiz Parrilla, commander of the San Saba presidio, led an army of about 600 presidial soldiers, volunteers, and Indian allies, including 134 Lipan Apaches, on a campaign of vengeance. Organized in San Antonio, the motley army marched to the presidio on the San Saba in late summer and headed northward. Fore-

37

warned local Indians fled from the army, and not until it had crossed the Clear Fork of the Brazos was it able to surprise a camp of Tonkawas. In an unequal battle, fifty-five Tonkawas were killed and 149 wounded without loss to the Spanish force. This was not vengeance enough for Ortiz, who continued northward, willingly guided by captured Tonkawas toward the fortified Wichita village on Red River. The Tonkawas, of course, may have been with malice aforethought leading the Spaniards into an ambush.

As the Spanish vanguard approached the wooded and brushy margins of the river, sixty to seventy warriors suddenly attacked it. The Wichitas lost three men in a brief skirmish and quickly retreated down a road into the forest. The Spaniards hotly pursued them down the road that abruptly ended in the open, sandy bottom land of the Red River opposite the fortified Taovaya village. Surprised and confused at the unexpected sight, the pursuers pulled back to consider what to do next. The village lay only a musket-shot away across the river, and the Spaniards could clearly see that a stockade and ditch protected part of the town of tall, oval-shaped lodges, and that the inhabitants of the rest of the village had crowded into the fortress. A winding, palisaded road, closed at the river with a gate, ran up the far bank to the fortress, and Wichitas equipped with muskets lined the stockade fence facing the attackers. On the left flank lay extensive, fenced fields of corn, beans, squash, and watermelons (probably introduced by

38

French traders). The Spaniards could also see corrals that held the Wichitas' horses, and behind them the tipis of the Comanches who had come to help their friends. In the center of the stockade, according to Ortiz, a French flag flew, and throughout the subsequent battle the Spaniards thought they heard a fife and drum.

Before the Spaniards could formulate a plan, Wichitas began to fire from the stockade. Others outside the palisades flanked the Spanish army both upriver and downriver, attempting unsuccessfully to surround it by getting between the forest and the attackers. The Spaniards had never seen Indians fight the way the Wichitas were fighting. Mounted warriors charged, fired their muskets, then retreated to be covered by foot soldiers, who also exchanged loaded muskets for the fired ones of the mounted men. The battle raged for about four hours, the Spaniards unable to reach the fortress, the Wichitas unable to overwhelm the Spaniards. The Spaniards did not know how many Indians they had engaged; some thought there were 6,000 enemy, others only 2,000, but all agreed that fresh contingents of Indians continued to arrive. Finally Ortiz was able to bring his two cannons into action, but the cannonade was ineffective — in fact the Indians laughed and mocked at their efforts. Again the Indians made a determined effort to surround the Spaniards. To prevent it the Spaniards had to retreat. Fortunately for them night was falling, and although the withdrawal did not turn into a rout, the cannons and much baggage were abandoned. The next day the army quickly took up the march toward the presidio on the San Saba. The Spaniards counted fifty-two men dead, wounded, or missing. Ortiz estimated that in addition to a particularly courageous Wichita chief, clad in white leather, more than fifty other Wichitas had been killed.

Some may argue that the battle was more of a standoff than a Spanish defeat, but however viewed, Ortiz retreated in haste and disorder. He had demonstrated, it is true, that Spanish armies could penetrate deep into the Indian heartland of the southern plains, but the Spaniards also learned that the Indians of the plains, equipped with horses and firearms, could and would meet the Spaniards in battle on something very close to equal terms. In larger perspective, Ortiz's campaign marks the beginning of the end of Spanish power in the southern plains, as it also marks the high tide of Wichita strength.

About the time that the Taovayas established their palisaded village on the Red River, Tawakonis and some Iscanis apparently settled on the upper Sabine River in northeast Texas. The Kichais and probably other Wichita divisions had long been familiar with this region and perhaps some had lived there, so that they were not moving to a totally strange land. Whether or not the Tawakonis and Iscanis were involved in the battle on the Red River is debatable. In any case, through Caddo intermediaries, they soon approached the Spaniards in east Texas with overtures of peace. The principal chief of the

40

Tawakonis even went to Nacogdoches and agreed to peace terms which included return of the captured cannons, cessation of hostilities with Apaches, and surrendering any who attacked missionaries or other Spaniards. The chief urged Fray Joseph de Calahorra, the veteran missionary at Nacogdoches, to visit his village.

It may seem odd that the Wichitas should seek peace with a nation that had just attacked them, but they had substantial reasons for seeking Spanish friendship. The only Europeans they had had dealings with in many years were Frenchmen, and these had been pleasant and profitable. They had no reason to believe that a Spanish association would be less successful. Their French contacts, so far as is known, did not oppose it, and may even have been for it. The Wichitas also needed allies; Osages had driven the Wichitas from their northern homeland and continued to menace their northern flank. The Wichitas could ill afford an even more formidable foe on their southern frontier. There may also have been an element of jealousy in their desire for friendship with the Spaniards; if a mission could be established for the hated Apaches, why not the Wichitas?

As a result of the Tawakoni request, Fray Calahorra, with a small retinue of soldiers and settlers, joined along the way by about one hundred Caddoes, visited the twin Tawakoni-Iscani village on the Sabine in the fall of 1760. The Spaniards were met about ten miles from the village and escorted to it, where four chiefs welcomed them. The entire

41

populace turned out to make signs of peace and warmly greeted these curious looking foreigners. Calahorra and his party remained in tipis especially prepared for them for eight days, exchanging presents and being feted and feasted in turn by the four chiefs.

Only a street separated the Tawakoni and Iscani towns, which Calahorra described as including forty-seven large dwellings, each housing twelve families. The towns had 250 warriors. Again, the *okonitsas* had performed their duties admirably. In Calahorra's words:

> The towns are located on a beautiful meadow . . . and are beautifully arranged with both streets and gardens. Their pasture lands are abundant, are common property, and produce fine breeding horses. Their farm lands, which they prohibit other tribes from using, are black and firm, and are maintained perhaps at a distance of a league from the town. They are accustomed to plant at the proper season all together in one labor. They gather in great abundance their products of maize, beans, and pumpkins and immediately divide them up into equal parts. They were constructing a fort or subterranean passage so they could defend themselves from the Spaniards or any other nation.

While at the Sabine River towns Calahorra met with a Taovaya chief, accompanied by twenty men and six women, who represented the Red River villages. Re-establishment of peaceful relations, including return of the two cannons and peace with the

Apaches was discussed, and Calahorra agreed to visit them the following summer in order to establish closer bonds and good relations.

Calahorra was unable to keep his word. He made a second visit to the Tawakoni-Iscani villages the next fall, and was given an even more cordial reception, but he was an old man and his failing health would not permit him to continue on to the Red River villages. During his eight-day visit Calahorra conferred certificates of captaincy, and canes symbolizing that office, on Chief *El Flechado en la Cara* of the Tawakonis and Chief *Llaso* or *Zurdo* ("Lefty") of the Iscanis, while an interpreter explained to them the nature of their new association and "submission" to Spanish authority. The ceremony was concluded by the distribution of presents among the populace. The symbols of office for the Taovaya chief and the gifts for his people were left with the Tawakonis and Iscanis, but the departure of Calahorra and his men was strained. The Wichitas were determined to have the Spaniards live with them and establish a mission, and it was difficult for them to understand why Calahorra would not comply with their wishes. The Spaniards were allowed to depart only after Calahorra had promised to return to live with them and begin a mission.

Calahorra immediately recommended to the governor to establish a mission for the Tawakoni-Iscani by abandoning the Apache mission. A settled, industrious people, already skilled farmers, the Wichitas were eager to have it and should be easy to convert.

A WICHITA CAMP showing a grass-thatched house, grass-thatched shade, and a tipi-pole-
previous growing season. The drying pole frame in front of the grass-thatched house, as well
centuries ago worked out an efficient technological adjustment to the southern Plains

frame, with an intensively-cultivated field in the foreground showing plants from the as the grass-thatching, indicates the long cultural stability of the people called Wichita, who environment.

Calahorra's recommendations were still struggling through the bureaucratic thicket the next fall (1762) when the Wichitas expected him to return.

During the same period Captain Rábago, then commander at the San Saba presidio, had strengthened the fort and made every effort to induce the Apaches to settle down. He even dispatched Spanish soldiers to escort them on their bison hunts, a practice that did not escape the notice of the Wichitas and other *Norteños*. Late in 1761, one Lipan Apache band succumbed to Rábago's blandishments and agreed to settle in a mission. The Apaches refused to settle on the San Saba, instead dictating a location about one hundred miles to the south on the upper Nueces River, at present Camp Wood. So it was that in January, 1762, a new but unauthorized mission, San Lorenzo de la Santa Cruz, was founded for the Lipan Apaches, and soon afterward a second mission was founded a few miles down the Nueces for another Lipan band.

In December, 1762, when Fray Calahorra failed to establish the promised mission for them, the Tawakonis and Iscanis sent three of their chiefs to Mission Nacogdoches after him. He could not accommodate the insistent Wichitas, and it was not until the next summer that he was able to obtain permission, the necessary supplies, and an escort to again visit them. They still wanted a mission and were cordial to Calahorra and his party, but the Taovaya delegation he met there was not. They had experienced three years of empty Spanish promises,

46

and no Spaniard had even visited them. They were openly critical of the Spaniards, although still interested in having Calahorra visit them, as they had brought along horses to transport the Spaniards to the Red River. Calahorra could not go with them, but he did promise to support their request.

The *Norteños* had soon discovered the new missions on the Nueces; they destroyed a Lipan camp near San Lorenzo in March, 1762, attacked another in May, and made another raid in July. They did not attack the missions, but that summer Taovayas raided the horse herd of the San Saba presidio, making off with seventy horses and killing three Spaniards. Their Tawakoni relatives objected to this breach of the peace, and hostilities between the two Wichita peoples developed over the matter.

As the Apaches fell or were thrown back, the Taovayas and other *Norteños* were enticed ever closer to the Spanish settlements. More conflicts with the Spaniards became inevitable and in the fall of 1763 *Norteños* raided San Antonio; and ominously, threatened to return in the spring. Spanish reinforcements were dispatched to San Antonio, among them a contingent of soldiers from Los Adaes in east Texas; it included Antonio Treviño. Then the *Norteños* did not attack San Antonio in the spring or summer of 1764; instead they seem to have pursued their Lipan enemies on the plains. That summer a beleaguered Captain Rábago at the San Saba presidio sought reinforcements. The soldiers from Los Adaes were sent there from San Antonio. It was while escorting

Apaches on a winter hunt in 1764 that Treviño was captured by Eyasiquiche.

Eyasiquiche, still interested in peace with the Spaniards, brought Treviño to the Tawakoni-Iscani village on the Sabine in the summer of 1765 on the eve of his departure for an expedition against the Osages. Two Iscanis escorted Eyasiquiche and his captive to Mission Nacogdoches. Father Calahorra, having nothing suitable in his poor mission for the distinguished visitor, suggested that Eyasiquiche accompany him to Los Adaes to visit Governor Martos.

Impatient to get on with his expedition, Eyasiquiche politely declined to go. Father Calahorra quickly sent a message to Governor Martos requesting aid; the governor understood the urgency of his message, and dispatched three horses to replace the worn out mounts Eyasiquiche and his party had ridden into Nacogdoches, as well as sending the best presents he could find on short notice.

In his talks with Calahorra, Eyasiquiche was blunt: the Taovayas did not want war with the Spaniards, but his people would not halt their attacks on the Apaches, because the Apaches continued to attack them and steal their horses, then often fleeing to the Spaniards for protection. Not only was Eyasiquiche returning Treviño to demonstrate his peaceful inclinations, but if the Spaniards came to the village on the Red River they could reclaim a number of captives and their cannons — which Frenchmen had shown the Wichitas how to use. Calahorra asked

48

Eyasiquiche if the Taovayas would still settle in a mission, granting that the Taovayas had the option of selecting the site. Eyasiquiche responded that he would have to consult his people on that question, strongly implying that they had lost interest in a mission. Ironically, while their discussions were in progress, Apaches attacked the Tawakoni-Iscani village, killing and capturing a number of its residents and stealing horses, lending substance to Eyasiquiche's contentions.

At another time Eyasiquiche's diplomacy might have borne fruit, but in that summer of 1765 it was doomed to failure. Eyasiquiche never even received a response from the Spaniards. Governor Martos was on his way out of office, and he could initiate no action. Hugo O'Connor, who replaced him, was determined to break Texas' hostile Indians, and by the time he assumed office the Taovayas were definitely in this category.

In larger perspective, distant events were conspiring to have profound effects on the future of the Wichita people. In the summer of 1759, King Fernando VI of Spain died. His successor, King Carlos III, while a good administrator and an enlightened ruler for that era, needed a decade to study the problems of his empire and initiate new policies and actions. On the distant borderlands Spanish policies stagnated and initiative was paralyzed. Also in the fall of 1759, Quebec fell to the British, forewarning the French expulsion from North America, and the end of a commercial relationship that had become an integral part of the Wichita economy. In 1762, King Carlos accepted New Orleans and Louisiana from France and the Treaty of Paris in the following year confirmed the Mississippi River boundary between the claimed possessions of Spain and Great Britain. The northern borderlands of New Spain were weakly held and under attack, and the gift of added territory was not an unmixed blessing. The alternative, however, was to have aggressive Englishmen possess it, threatening Texas and Mexico.

As part of a comprehensive study, aimed at the reorganization of the military posture of New Spain brought on by the transfer of Louisiana to Spain, in 1767, the Marqués de Rubi made a tour of inspection of Texas. His subsequent recommendations marked a reversal in policy toward the Wichitas and other *Norteños*. He advocated a war of extermination against the Apaches and friendship with the *Norteños*. These recommendations came too late; the Wichitas were understandably wary of the Spaniards, and they no longer wanted missions among them. The recommendations were not implemented, and Spanish policies were soon again to run contrary to Wichita interests.

The actual transfer of Louisiana from France to Spain was not accomplished until 1769, and for a time the old trading relationships were not disturbed. French traders were licensed and permitted to continue their commerce. Thus, it was hoped that trade could continue uninterrupted and that the Spaniards

50

might inherit the goodwill the Indians felt for Frenchmen. It was not to be. The Spaniards were too rigid to make significant changes in their old policies. While firearms were traded to the *Norteños,* their numbers were restricted, imposing a heavy burden on peoples engaged in a desperate struggle with Osages, who had no such handicap. Indian slavery also was abolished in Louisiana, another blow to the economy of the Wichitas; for many years they had profitably bartered Apache captives to the French colonists. The licensed traders were also prohibited from buying horses and mules from the *Norteños,* inasmuch as most of them had been taken from Spanish settlements in New Mexico and Texas.

The impact of the new regulations was softened somewhat by Athanase de Mézierès, a Frenchman with long experience at the Natchitoches Post and skilled in Indian diplomacy. As lieutenant governor of Natchitoches, he was responsible for carrying out the new policies. He first allied himself with the nearby Caddo tribes, persuading them to remain peaceful, turn over unlicensed traders to the authorities, and not to supply the *Norteños* with arms. With their trade at Natchitoches cut off, the Wichitas turned to trading with illicit traders, but they were soon in difficult circumstances. By the summer of 1771, their need for European goods was such that the Wichitas agreed to peace on De Mézierès' terms, and that fall signed a treaty at Natchitoches. With trade more or less restored, frontier tensions subsided, and in the late winter of 1772 De Mézierès

51

visited a village of Wichita proper in order to strengthen the new alliance. The village was newly established on the upper Brazos River. Although there were numerous bison in the area, it was far from an ideal location in that it lacked wood for building and fuel.

De Mézierès soon realized that the danger of British influence among the Wichitas was substantial; the Taovayas had already received English trade goods through the Pawnees. The Osages also continued to be a threat; in fact, they attacked European settlements in Louisiana as well as Indian villages. Consequently, De Mézierès conceived the idea of arming the *Norteños*, and encouraging them to fight Osages, thus creating a buffer between the Osages and Louisiana, supplying the firearms the *Norteños* demanded. He also hoped to establish a presidio at the Wichita village on the Brazos, where the Taovayas had promised to move, thereby cementing the ties with the Wichitas and serving notice to the British of Spanish control of the area.

The Spanish government did not approve plans for the presidio; the Taovayas failed to move to the new location; and De Mézierès shortly left for a year's leave of absence in Europe. While he was gone, the fragile ties with the Spaniards came loose. The Taovayas were angry at the refusal of the Natchitoches traders to take their horses and captives, and De Mézierès had not fulfilled his promises. To make matters worse, Taovaya and Comanche war parties, returning from raids, reported that the Apaches were

52

using Spanish firearms. The Wichitas threatened war and increased their raiding in Texas, but what they most desired was to establish peaceful trade with the Spaniards. De Mézieres was able to calm the restive Wichitas when he returned to his post. For a time it even appeared that better days lay ahead after the northern provinces of New Spain were put into a single military department under Commander General Don Teodoro de Croix.

Croix resurrected De Mézieres' scheme for a campaign against the Apaches, using all the Spanish forces he could muster as well as *Norteño* warriors. The colonial government considered the scheme, was favorably inclined, and assigned De Mézieres the task of recruiting *Norteños* for it. He had already determined, while planning a campaign against the Osages, that they could raise 1,300 warriors over and above those needed to defend their villages.

De Mézieres chose the Taovaya village on the Red River as an ideal place to gather the Indian and Spanish forces, and while waiting for royal authorization for the campaign, De Mézieres, accompanied by Treviño, the former captive of the Taovayas, visited the villages in the spring of 1778. The Spaniards were received enthusiastically. De Mézieres distributed presents in the name of Croix and assured the Indians of Spanish protection. The Wichitas, for their part, began construction of a large house for the use of any Spaniards who might come to live in the village with them in the future, and they urged the Spaniards to settle nearby, insisting that they would

53

help in every way possible to get such a colony established. Moreover, the Wichitas readily surrendered the cannons they had held for so many years. At the time of the visit, there were thirty-seven lodges in the village on the north side of the river, 123 on the south side of the stream. There were 800 warriors in the two villages and a large number of women and children.

When De Mézierès was at the Wichita villages, the plan for the Apache campaign approved, but put off until more Spanish troops could be provided. The plan died permanently in 1779 when Croix was notified that no additional troops would be available. Spain had entered the War of the American Revolution, and all of its resources had to be diverted in the struggle against England. De Mézierès attempted to visit the Wichita villages again, but he sustained a severe injury and had to turn back. He never fully recovered and died in November, 1779.

The last two decades of the century saw a marked decline in the fortunes and strength of the Wichita peoples. De Mézierès had promised them annual presents, a resident trader in the Taovaya village, and generous prices for their goods. None of the promises was kept. By 1780, they were virtually out of ammunition, and many of their weapons were worn out or needed repair.

The Spaniards compounded the Wichitas' problems by inviting Choctaw, Chickasaw, and other Indians of the United States to move to Spanish-held territory, in order to create a buffer between themselves and the Osages, and to strengthen the border against American penetration. For the Wichitas it meant more competition in hunting and it was beneficial only in that these immigrant tribes were also enemies of the Osages. Epidemics had swept through the Wichita villages time and time again, with fearful mortality, the smallpox epidemics of 1788 and 1801 being particularly bad. Warfare, too, had taken its toll, so that by the beginning of the nineteenth century the Wichita peoples bore but a shadowy resemblance to the powerful people they once had been.

THE LOUISIANA PURCHASE
AND THE COMING OF THE AMERICANS

With the return of Louisiana to France and its subsequent sale to the United States in 1803, the Wichitas found themselves occupying both sides of an international border. The Taovayas and other northern Wichitas were already acquainted with American traders, whom they had welcomed in their villages. For a time they had hopes of reviving their languishing trade. Perhaps too, they looked forward to finding helpful American mentors and allies. They were to be disappointed. Americans knew little of the Wichitas and were preoccupied with their own affairs. The Wichitas were too few and scattered to draw much attention to themselves, or to pose a threat to American expansion.

In 1804, Dr. John Sibley, an American who lived in Natchitoches, Louisiana, was put in charge of the

55

Indian affairs of the neighboring region. His job was to learn what he could about the Indians, encourage trade with them, and gain their goodwill and cooperation. Sibley did not visit the Indians in their villages and camps, but veteran traders supplied him with much information about them, and delegations of Indians soon came to Natchitoches to trade, talk with him, and receive presents. By the spring of 1805, Sibley had acquired considerable information about the Wichitas in the Spanish Fort area. They were now governed by a single chief, Great Bear, who was a Wichita (Wichita proper). Sibley added that:

They have many horses and mules; they raise more corn, pumpkins, beans, and tobacco, than they want for their own consumption; the surplusage they exchange with the Hietans [Comanches], for buffalo rugs, horses, and mules; the pumpkins they cut round in their shreds, and when it is in a state of dryness, that it is so tough it will not break, but bend, they plat and work it into large mats, in which state they sell it to the Hietans [Comanches], who, as they travel, cut off, and eat it, as they want it. Their tobacco they manufacture and cut as fine as tea, which is put into leather bags of a certain size, and is, likewise, an article of trade. They have but few guns, and very little ammunition; what they have they keep for war, and hunt with the bow; their meat is principally buffalo; seldom kill a deer, though they are so plenty they come into their villages, and about their houses, like a domestic animal . . . The men go entirely

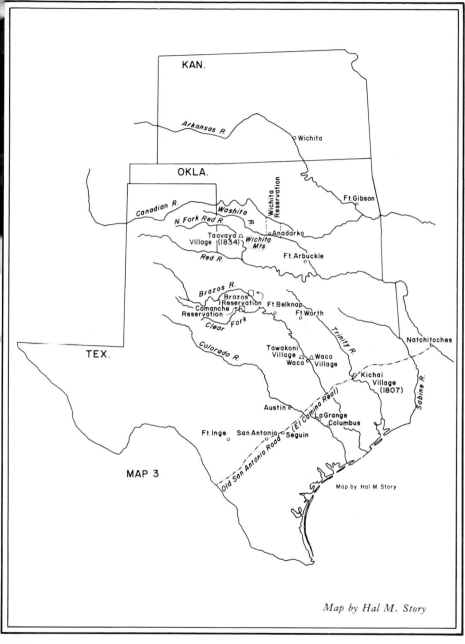

KAN.

Arkansas R.

Wichita

OKLA.

Canadian R.

Washita

N. Fork Red R.

Wichita Reservation

Ft. Gibson

Taovaya Village (1834)

Wichita Mts.

Anadarko

Red R.

Ft. Arbuckle

Brazos R.

Brazos Reservation

Ft. Belknap

Comanche Reservation

Clear Fork

Ft. Worth

Natchitoches

TEX.

Colorado R.

Tawakoni Village

Waco

Waco Village

Trinity R.

Kichai Village (1807)

Sabine R.

Austin

La Grange

Columbus

(El Camino Real)

Ft. Inge

San Antonio

Seguin

MAP 3

Old San Antonio Road

Map by Hal M. Story

Map by Hal M. Story

MAP 3.

naked, and the women nearly so, only wearing a small flap, of a piece of skin. They have a number of Spaniards amongst them, of a fair complexion, taken from the settlement of Santa Fe when they were children, who live as they do, and have no knowledge of where they came from . . . Their present number of men is estimated at about four hundred. A great number of them, four years ago, were swept off by the small pox.

It was not until the early summer of 1807 that a Taovaya chief and eight companions, with a drove of horses to trade, accompanied by two American traders who had been in their Red River villages, journeyed to Natchitoches to see Sibley. It was the first official contact between an agent of the United States government and the Wichitas. The traders reported that the Spanish governor at San Antonio was still attempting to ingratiate himself with the Taovayas. They had accepted presents from the Spaniards, but their paramount chief had refused to allow the Spanish colors to be flown in the Spanish Fort villages. They already flew the colors of the United States in one village, and they requested two more flags so that each village could be similarly equipped. The delegation was given presents by Sibley, and they presumably traded their drove of horses.

Later that summer delegations of Tawakonis, Wichitas, and Kichais also visited Sibley. They complained of the high prices that American traders were charging, bewailed the problems they had with the Osages, and informed Sibley of the plentiful supply of horses and mules, bison hides, and other things they had to trade. They were friendly, wanted peace with the Americans, and even those who lived in Spanish Texas vowed that they would live in peace and friendship with the Americans.

Perhaps a profitable trade might have been developed with the Americans, at least at the Spanish Fort villages, but this did not occur. The demand for the things the Wichitas had for barter could readily be supplied elsewhere. The Spanish Fort villages were so remote and frequently harassed by Osages, that they were probably not attractive to resident traders. Had the Indian trade been run by the government the story might have been different, but Sibley could not impose his wishes on private traders. Unfortunately, too, in 1811, the paramount chief of the Spanish Fort villages died on his way home from a visit to Natchitoches. The Wichita would not or could not agree on a successor; not only did the old subdivisions reassert their independence, but the Taovayas also split up, some retreating to the safety of the Wichita Mountains, others joining the Tawakonis in Texas. As a result, the strategically located villages on the Red River were no longer continuously occupied. Their abandonment spelled the failure of the commercial aspirations of the Wichitas.

TROUBLES IN SPANISH TEXAS

In the early years of the century, the various other Wichita subdivisions continued to inhabit scattered villages in Spanish Texas. The Kichais, who had

59

long maintained their independence and separate identity, had moved southward from the headwaters of the Sabine to the lower Trinity River. When Sibley first heard of them, their small village (counting sixty warriors) was on the east bank of that stream just above the Old San Antonio Road *(El Camino Real)*. The Tawakonis and Iscanis had also abandoned their joint village on the Sabine during the last years of the eighteenth century, moving south-westward to the valley of the Brazos River in central Texas. The Tawakonis established a village on the east side of the river, the Iscanis a village on the west bank several miles above the Tawakoni village; both were in the environs of present-day Waco.

Sibley did not mention the Iscanis in his early communications, but in a newspaper article, published about 1820, he referred to them as "Whacoes." Other Americans and Texans also invariably used the term "Waco," spelling and probably pronouncing it in a variety of ways. There were at this time, according to Sibley, 350-400 Wacos, 230-250 Tawakonis, 130-150 Kichais, and 500-600 Taovayas and Wichitas in the Spanish Fort villages. The total population of between 1,200 and 1,400 people represented a tremendous decline from earlier days.

The early decades of the nineteenth century were a hectic, confused time for the Wichitas in Texas. Mexican revolutionaries, American filibusters, immigrant Indians from the east, and no doubt others managed to embroil them in their varied

60

schemes and activities. Few, if any of them, benefited the Wichitas, but none seem to have been disastrous either. It was not until the establishment of Anglo-American colonies in southeastern Texas under Spanish grants, in the 1820's, and the successful revolution that made Mexico independent, that the southerly Wichita villages were confronted with aggressive, uncompromising, and often hostile neighbors, who were soon to cause them to move again.

The Wacos first came to the attention of Stephen F. Austin's colonists in the summer of 1823, when returning from a battle with Tonkawas, they were seen camped on the Colorado River near La Grange. The next spring, a large party of Wacos, hunting for Tonkawa, frightened settlers near present Columbus, and were assumed to have killed a settler near present-day Seguin. In retaliation, settlers surprised and killed twelve Wacos. That same spring a group of Mexicans stole horses from the Wacos and drove them through Austin's colony. Pursuing Wacos indemnified themselves by appropriating a considerable number of the settlers' horses. Thus was inaugurated the kind of behavior that typified Texan-Wichita relations for many years: friction, misunderstanding, Indian raids, settler and ranger pursuit, and retaliation.

Austin's struggling colony could ill afford continued conflict with the Wichitas, and Austin sent commissioners to the Brazos villages to "form a lasting treaty of peace and friendship for ever." Thomas M. Duke, one of the commissioners, re-

61

ported that there were sixty houses in the Waco village, with about 400 acres of corn, beans, pumpkins, and melons under cultivation. The Tawakoni village had only seven houses, and Duke also learned that the Wichita proper lived on the Brazos about six days' travel above the Waco village. Most of the Wacos were away on a hunt, but Duke delivered what might be described as a friendly warning to the few Wacos who remained at home. Hostilities continued despite Duke's visit, and the Mexican government in August, 1825, ordered Austin to destroy the Waco village. Austin procrastinated, but finally, in the spring of 1826, invited immigrant Cherokees, who were at odds with the Wichitas, to join in a campaign against them. It did not materialize, as the government rescinded its order, but it served to encourage the Cherokees to attack the Wichitas.

With the Anglo-American population of Texas increasing rapidly, and settlements pushing ever closer to their relatively small villages, there was little the Wichitas could do to hold on to their lands. The young men carried on a kind of guerilla warfare, raiding white settlements and ranches, stealing horses primarily, to be pursued by hastily organized parties of settlers or rangers. They sometimes lost the horses as well as their lives. The most damaging blows, however, seem to have come from the Cherokees, who in the spring of 1829 made a surprise attack on the Waco village. They did not overwhelm it, as the Wacos retreated to an earthen fort and Tawakoni reinforcements arrived to help, but a

62

considerable number of its inhabitants were killed. The next summer an even larger force of Cherokees attacked a small, off-shoot Tawakoni village that had been established about thirty miles to the east, near Tehuacana, Limestone County. The Cherokees were reported to have overwhelmed it, only a few women and children surviving.

The Kichais did not come into conflict with Texans as quickly as the Wacos and Tawakonis, but in 1835, they were accused of committing "depredations." After a fight at their village with a party of Texans, they fled to the forks of the Trinity River, hundreds of miles to the northwest.

LAND CESSION AND THE DRAGOON EXPEDITION

While not faced with the settlement of Americans in their lands in the early decades of the century, the more northerly Taovayas and Wichitas were confronted with a different and equally serious problem they were helpless to combat. The United States government after 1818 pursued a policy of removing surviving Indians of the eastern states to land acquired by the Louisiana Purchase. These lands were, of course, already occupied. The government attempted to solve this problem by negotiating land cessions with tribes that inhabited, or were thought to inhabit them. Unfortunately for the Wichitas, the Quapaws of Arkansas ceded to the United States a tremendous strip of territory running from the Mississippi westward between the Arkansas and Canadian on the north, to the Red River on the south, westward to the source of the Canadian. The Quapaws had never occupied and probably had no acquaintance with the western half or two-thirds of this land. It had been the homeland of the Wichitas, and they still lived in parts of it.

By the Treaty of Doak's Stand in 1820, the Choctaws were persuaded to trade their ancient homeland in the southeastern United States for the lands ceded by the Quapaws, and in 1830 the Treaty of Dancing Rabbit Creek reaffirmed their title to the lands between the Red and Canadian Rivers. How quickly the Wichitas learned that their lands had been given to others is not recorded. In any case, intruding Indians were not welcome. The Wichitas, few in numbers and short of firearms, could not prevent their intrusion, but their allies, the Kiowas and Comanches, were still formidable. Together they made the western plains a dangerous place for Choctaws and other eastern Indians.

Realizing that the western tribes were opposed to the invasion of their lands by eastern Indians, and hoping to demonstrate the strength of the United States its officials dispatched, in the summer of 1834, a dragoon regiment under Colonel Henry Dodge to visit the western tribes, including the people known as the "Pawnee Picts." Dodge had no idea where the Pawnee Pict village was. After he passed through the Cross Timbers, he encountered a band of Comanches, who led the dragoons to their camp for a friendly visit. The Comanches were not familiar with Dodge's term for the Wichitas, but he

64

soon learned that the Comanches called them "Toyash" (Taovaya), and that their new village lay beyond the Wichita Mountains, which were visible to the southwest.

After taking a round-about course, the dragoons camped on July 20 within a few miles of the village, and the next day were escorted to it by its friendly but wary inhabitants. The village of some 200 lodges was located in Devil's Canyon on the North Fork of the Red River (near present Lugert, Oklahoma). Fenced and well-cultivated fields extended for several miles along the valley, and the dragoons found the grass covered lodges, the largest with a diameter of forty feet and a height of thirty feet, to be comfortable homes. The Taovayas were hospitable hosts, entertaining the officers with feasts of corn, beans, watermelons, and wild plums. Their provisions having run desperately low, the soldiers carried on an active trade with their hosts for green corn, dried bison and horse flesh.

Not only were talks held with the Taovayas, but Comanches and Kiowa delegations attended, as well as representatives from a nearby Waco village, lately arrived from Texas. Dodge suggested that the Indians make peace with their ancient Osage enemies and with the tribes the government was moving to the west. The government, according to Dodge, was prepared to guarantee the peace, send traders, and provide cattle, so that the Indians would have a continuing supply of meat after the bison were gone. Dodge's proposals were affirmed by the Cherokee,

65

Osage, and Delaware delegations that had accompanied the expedition.

The proposals were appealing, but the western tribes were reluctant to send delegations into the lands of their ancient enemies to make treaties. Dodge finally persuaded Comanche, Kiowa, Taovaya, and Waco delegations to return with him to Fort Gibson, and all did, save the Comanches, whose delegation soon deserted. Early in September they met at Fort Gibson with Osage, Cherokee, Creek, Choctaw, and Seneca representatives. Although Colonel Dodge did not have the authority to make peace treaties, the conference was a friendly one, and the groundwork was laid for another council the following year. The Wichitas persuaded their Comanche friends to attend this council, and on August 25, 1835, the tribes met with United States commissioners at Camp Holmes on the Canadian River (near Lexington, Oklahoma), and agreed to peace and perpetual friendship with one another and with the United States. It was the first treaty of the Wichitas with the United States, and it established the usage of "Wichita" for the Wichita peoples.

INDIAN POLICIES OF THE REPUBLIC OF TEXAS

After the establishment of the Republic of Texas in 1836, thanks partly to a free land policy, settlers flocked to Texas. The Kichais, Tawakonis, and Wacos had already fled from their old villages in the lower valleys of the Trinity and Brazos, as we have seen, but renewed conflict with Texans was not long

66

SKYSEROKA, a secondary chief of the people called Wichita in 1834, when he was sketched by artist George Catlin. Accompanying United States Dragoons to the "Pawnee Pict" settlement, Catlin characterized Skyseroka as "a remarkably clever man, and much approved and valued in his tribe." From *Letters and Notes on the Manners, Customs, and Conditions of the North American Indians*. Vol. II, Plate 175, 1841.

avoided. In its first years of existence, under the leadership of Sam Houston, the Republic pursued a policy of peace and conciliation with its Indians. When Mirabeau B. Lamar replaced Houston as President in December of 1838, however, a policy designed to expel, defeat, or exterminate all Indians within the borders of the Republic was adopted; conflicts were already increasing.

In the fall of 1837, a group of Texans fought a battle on the headwaters of the Trinity River with a force of 150 Kichai, Waco, Wichita proper, and Caddoes. The Texans lost their horses and ten men were killed and three wounded; they estimated that they killed sixty Indians. Commissioners were dispatched to make peace, and in September, 1838, Kichai, Tawakoni, Taovaya, and Waco chiefs concluded their first peace treaty with the Republic. Then Lamar replaced Houston, the Texas Senate did not ratify the treaty, and sporadic conflict continued on the upper Trinity and Brazos. The Wichita slowly retreated northward, hoping to find good locales where they could settle peaceably. This was to prove impossible, and there was little the out-numbered, outgunned warriors could do, save carry on a kind of guerrilla warfare, sending small parties into the settlements to raid and drive off horses. Waco warriors in particular became famous as adept horse thieves, the best on the Texas frontier.

Houston was returned to the presidency of the Republic in December, 1841. He resumed a conciliatory Indian policy, but it was by then virtually impossible to persuade any Indians of the peaceful inclinations of the government. Nevertheless, Houston appointed agents for the tribes, who were to endeavor to persuade them to meet in council and to sign treaties of friendship. He also employed a small group of Delaware Indians, who were familiar with the Comanches, Wichitas, and other "wild" tribes, to serve as guides, interpreters, and mediators. They were the key to reopening the channels of communication.

It was not until March, 1843, however, that some of the smaller and normally friendly tribes could be persuaded to assemble at the Tehuacana Creek council grounds, near modern Waco, and then it was only to agree to a truce and to promise to attend a council in the fall. Acaquash, the second chief of the Wacos, though not authorized to make an agreement for his own people, signed for them as well as the other Wichita subdivisions. Houston was persistent in his efforts, and in the next year various Wichita subdivisions participated in a number of rather tentative councils with the Texans. These conferences hardly altered the precarious Wichita situation.

Finally, in October, 1844, virtually all of the indigenous and immigrant tribes of Texas gathered at the Tehuacana Creek council ground. The council was successful in that the Indians agreed to peace, and to meet annually to confer with the Texans and receive presents. Through the insistence of Buffalo Hump, a leading Southern Comanche chief, the boundary line that Houston proposed to run between the Indians and Texas had to be stricken from the treaty. The Texas Senate ratified the treaty, and Anson Jones, who succeeded Houston, signed it on February 5, 1845.

Neither Wichitas nor Comanches showed up on time the following fall to talk with the Texans, but when the Wichitas finally appeared they had the Wichita proper with them, a sub-tribe that had absented itself from earlier councils. A treaty of friendship was concluded, identical to the one of the previous year, and the first between Wichita of the United States and Texas, and the last treaty of the Republic of Texas with the Wichitas.

PROBLEMS OF STATEHOOD

In a few weeks Texas was annexed to the United States. It came at a time when Houston's policy of peace was beginning to bear fruit, but however beneficial statehood was for Texans, it spelled doom for its Indians. All public lands were reserved to the state, although they had hardly been defined, let alone explored, and they had never been transferred by sale or gift by their Indian inhabitants. Whatever shadowy obligations Texans may have felt for the Indians were transferred to the federal government by annexation. Henceforward many Texans would clamor loudly for the removal or extermination of these government wards who occupied "their" lands.

With annexation in the offing and hostilities with Mexico likely, the federal government designated commissioners to make new treaties with the state's

70

Indians. It was the spring of 1846 before all of the scattered Indians could be gathered at the Tehuacana Creek council grounds. The elaborate fourteen article treaty that resulted broke no new ground. Many of the Indians were almost totally ignorant of the nation which had now imposed its authority over them, however imperfectly, and it appears that many of them did not understand that the disliked Texans had become Americans through the mysteries of annexation. Representatives of all the Wichita subdivisions put their X's to the treaty.

The treaty was not ratified by the Senate nor signed by President Polk until March, 1847, so the promised presents for the Indians were delayed. More false promises, it must have seemed, and there was frustration and anger in the Wichita villages.

Some Wichitas set themselves up as middlemen, trading merchandise and particularly horses that had been stealthily acquired in the Texas settlements, to Indian and white traders in Indian Territory. That this did not result in reprisals probably should be credited to Major Robert S. Neighbors, former Indian agent for the Republic of Texas. Sympathetic, fair, and able, he became U.S. Special Agent for the Texas Indians. As soon as the treaty was ratified, he purchased presents on credit and set out for the Waco and Tawakoni villages, then on the Brazos River near its junction with the Clear Fork. After three days of talks he persuaded the Tawakonis and Wacos to halt their depredations and return all horses and mules stolen since the treaty was signed.

71

By staying in Indian country and by distributing presents, Neighbors was able to keep an unsteady peace with most of the Wichita and other Brazos River tribes. Following the conclusion of the Mexican War in February, 1848, however, Texas saw a rapid growth of population and westward expansion. After the legislature asked Congress in 1848 for protection from Indians, a series of posts and forts were built and garrisoned from Fort Worth on the Trinity River in the north to Fort Inge on the southwest. So rapidly did settlers push beyond the chain of forts that in 1850 the legislature again demanded protection for its people. In 1851, sites for new forts were selected well beyond the frontier, and a half dozen were constructed, from Fort Belknap on the Brazos to Fort Clark in the south. They were monuments to the dispossession of the Indians.

THE TEXAS RESERVATIONS

There seemed to be little room in Texas for Indians, but for a time it appeared that they might be assigned permanent homes. At the urging of Neighbors, the legislature passed a bill authorizing the federal government to provide Indian reserves on unoccupied Texas land. Neighbors and United States Army Captain R. B. Marcy selected the sites. One, for the Comanches, was on the Clear Fork of the Brazos; the other, for the Wacos, Tawakonis, and several other small tribes, consisted of 46,080 acres on the Brazos in present Young County. The hard-pressed Wichitas must have received with relief and

Courtesy Caldwell Collection, Humanities Research Center, University of Texas
BUFFALO-GOAD, Chief of the Waco Tribe, photographed about 1875 by William Soule, photographer at Fort Sill.

renewed hope the news that they had been given land for permanent homes. The Indians began moving onto the reserves in January, 1855, and the Wacos and Tawakonis quickly established farming villages.

Although the Wichitas and other Indians on the Brazos Reserve, and the Comanches on the Clear Fork were peaceful, committing no depredations, nearby Texas settlers were so hostile and menacing that by June, 1859, the federal government planned to abandon the Texas reservations. On the first of August, 1,050 Indians, including approximately 375 Wacos and Tawakonis, left the reserve. The army escorted them north across the Red River to the Leased District in Indian Territory. They were nearly destitute and landless.

THE RUSH CREEK MASSACRE

By 1859, the condition of the Wichitas in the Leased District of Indian Territory was hardly any better than that of the refugees from Texas. About 900 Wichitas and 300 Kichais lived in a village on Rush Creek. They were asked by government officials to persuade the Comanches to come in to Fort Arbuckle for a council, and they did so. The Comanche band started for the fort, and on the way stopped to visit their friends at Rush Creek. While there, on October 1, 1858, four companies of cavalry under Major Earl Van Dorn, with 125 Indians from the Texas reserve, attacked them without warning. Van Dorn's expedition had departed from Fort

74

Belknap in Texas, proceeded to the Wichita Mountains where he learned that the Comanches were camped near the Wichita village. He followed them there, unaware that they were peacefully coming in for a parley.

The Comanches fought desperately, but after losing some fifty-three of their number, fled. The Wichita village of 120 lodges was burned, and their food, crops, and possessions, including most of their horses, were destroyed or lost. Fearing that the Comanches believed the attack was brought on by their treachery, the destitute Wichitas fled to Fort Arbuckle. They had no choice but to remain at the fort that winter, protected and fed by the government.

In the spring of 1859, Elias Rector, Superintendent of the Southern Superintendency, and Samuel A. Blain, agent for the Wichita and Affiliated Bands (Kichais, Caddoes, and Delawares) were authorized to select a site for an agency and land for a reservation. Rector, the Wichita, Kichai, and Caddo headmen, a group of Delawares, and a military escort set out to find a suitable location. They first went to the site of the old Wichita village on Cache Creek, but Rector found it unacceptable for the agency, because it was militarily indefensible and the Wichitas had suffered much from malaria in this location. The party then proceeded to the old Kichai village, situated some forty miles to the north on the Washita River. Here was good grass and timber, and the agency was located on the south side of the river on the site of the old village; the Wichitas picked out land to the north for their homes.

In July, Agent Blain moved the Wichitas from Fort Arbuckle to their new home along the Washita, and they were soon joined by the Wichitas from the Texas reserve. Grass lodges were quickly erected. By the next summer 141 acres had been fenced and were under cultivation, but the most severe drought in thirty years ruined the crops. The people had to continue to depend upon the frequently inadequate, poor-quality rations the agency issued.

THE CIVIL WAR

The Wichitas were hardly settled in their new homes before they were caught up in the cataclysm of the Civil War. In the spring of 1861, the troops stationed at Forts Arbuckle, Washita, and Cobb were ordered to Fort Leavenworth, Kansas, leaving the Wichitas and the other Indians of the Leased District to fend for themselves. Confederate troops from Texas occupied the abandoned forts, and Agent Leeper, a Texan, was retained in his old post after he took an oath of allegiance to the Confederacy. The Confederacy sent Albert Pike to the Leased District to make treaties with its Indians, but despite the arguments and threats that were used, the Wichitas refused to sign a treaty. Their memory of Texas and Texans was too fresh. A fraudulent pact was ultimately signed, however, by three Wichitas under duress; it was repudiated by the Wichitas after the war was concluded.

76

The Wichitas, understandably, received few favors from the Confederacy, but no troops were sent to intimidate or harass them — or to protect Agent Leeper. The agent was unpopular, and the young men and warriors made his life miserable, insulting him, killing the agency stock, and causing problems by stealing horses in the vicinity, and apparently as far away as Texas.

In the fall of 1862, a Delaware and Shawnee Indian force from Kansas made its way south into Texas, then turned north, and after nightfall on October 23, surrounded the Wichita Agency buildings. Subsequent events are somewhat confused, but the buildings were burned and some of the agency employees killed. After the marauders had set fire to the buildings, the force trailed a body of Tonkawas, who had been at the agency, and in the morning massacred them.

What, if any part, the Wichitas played in the attack on the agency is unknown; in any case, the marauding Indians did not attack them. Fearful that Confederate forces bent on retaliation would do so, the bulk of the Wichitas and other agency Indians fled to Kansas. A temporary Wichita agency was established at Belmont, Kansas, and the Wichitas spent the rest of the winter along the Verdigris and Fall Rivers near the agency. Again they had been driven into headlong flight, and they arrived in Kansas nearly destitute and without resources. In the following summer of 1863, they moved to the mouth of the Little Arkansas River, where there was good hunting. Their temporary village is now in the heart of the city of Wichita, ironically perpetuating the name of this refugee camp, not the fact that their ancestors once possessed these rich Arkansas valley lands.

The war years in Kansas were difficult and damaging for the Wichitas. There was much sickness in the fall of 1863, and in the next year smallpox struck down a number of people, and several times the crops were ruined by floods. The end of the war in 1865 meant that the Wichitas could be better supplied by the government, but a new agent, Henry Shanklin, appointed in the fall of 1866, reported that they still were poorly fed and clothed, many were sick, and they were despondent and demoralized. While a few Wichitas may have been absent, a census revealed a total of only 822 persons. The government had intended to move the Wichitas back to the Leased District that year, but for a variety of reasons it was put off until the summer of 1867. High water postponed their departure that summer, but worse, cholera broke out a few days before they were to leave and exacted a terrible toll. By that fall most of the surviving Wichitas were finally back on the Washita. It marked the end of many migrations; they were home at last.

RECENT HISTORY

Although the Wichitas returned to their old homes along the Washita, they were unable to secure government recognition of their right to its possession. It was part of the Leased District the Choctaws and Chickasaws ceded to the government in the summer of 1868. The southern half was allocated to the Kiowas, Comanches, and Apaches, and the following summer, by the executive order of President Grant, the Cheyennes and Arapahoes were located on the remainder. Again, it appeared, the Wichitas had been dispossessed.

Then in February, 1870, the Secretary of the Interior approved a recommendation of the Office of Indian Affairs, that a permanent reservation be set aside for the Wichita as near to their old home as possible. That May the Wichitas agreed to accept a reservation bound on the east by the 98th meridian between the Canadian and Washita Rivers; it included the old reservation lands as designated by Superintendent Rector in 1859. The Indian appropriation act of 1872 tacitly recognized that the Wichitas had been placed on a reservation, and it also provided funds for a Wichita delegation to travel to Washington. That fall in Washington, the commissioner concluded an agreement with the nine Wichita delegates that granted to the Wichita and Affiliated Bands, a somewhat larger reservation than had been agreed to, extending between the main channels of the Washita and Canadian, westward from the 98th degree of longitude to 98 degrees 40 minutes. The tract embraced 743,257 acres. In return, the Wichita relinquished all claims of any kind to lands in Texas, Louisiana, Indian Territory, and elsewhere. The agreement was transmitted to Congress

A WICHITA MID-19TH CENTURY ENCAMPMENT with tipi housing, photographed by William

Courtesy Smithsonian Institution, Bureau of American Ethnology

S. Soule between 1867 and 1874.

for ratification in January, 1873, but it was not then, or ever, ratified.

The Wichitas stubbornly resisted the determined efforts of the Cherokee Commission, under the provisions of the General Allotment Act (Dawes Act) of February 8, 1887, to break up their reservation, even though their title to it was clouded. They were for a time denied legal counsel, and were offered only about fifty cents an acre for their "surplus" land. Led by their chief, Tawakoni Jim, they defended themselves as best they could, and adamantly refused to part with any of their land for less than $1.25 an acre. The Wichitas were, however, confronted with an overwhelming force determined and able to take their lands. They were told, for example, that if they did not accept individual allotments of 160 acres, the commission would cut the allotments in half. Ultimately, under these and other threats, on June 4, 1891, 152 Wichitas out of an adult male population of 227, signed what they thought was an agreement to sell the western half of their reservation, keeping the remainder intact. They still rejected the commission's offer of fifty cents an acre for the land; it was agreed that the price to be paid for it would be left up to Congress.

By the fall of 1893, the Wichitas had discovered that the agreement they signed applied to all their land, and they petitioned Congress asking that the agreement be rejected unless they were paid at least $1.25 for their surplus land. In the meantime the agreement had been transmitted to Congress by

82

President Harrison, but Congress did not get around to ratifying it until March 2, 1895. The amount of compensation the Wichitas were to receive was passed on to the Court of Claims, because the Choctaw and Chickasaw claim to the land was still in dispute. On January 9, 1899, the Court of claims delivered the opinion that the Wichitas were entitled to allotments as provided in the agreement but that the Choctaws and Chickasaws were owners of the surplus land. Several years later, on December 10, 1900, the Supreme Court reversed the Court of Claims, thus leading to allotment in severalty, compensation of $1.25 an acre for surplus land, and the opening of the reservation. Allotments were made to 963 Indians by July 1, 1901, and the land-holdings of the Wichitas and Affiliated Bands were thereby reduced by almost 600,000 acres.

By the last decade of the century the future seemed bleak and hopeless. The Wichitas were no longer a powerful, independent people, but a poor, subjugated remnant. All too obviously the old life and the old ways were fast slipping away, and in the depths of despair they realized that there was nothing they could do in any practical sense to change their condition, or to turn the clock back to a better, happier day. Yet there remained another way, a way that other peoples suffering through similar national or tribal crises have often seized, and one that the Indians of the plains, including the Wichitas, fervently grasped. It was known as the "Ghost Dance."

The Ghost Dance religion of 1890 was initiated

83

by Wovoka, a Paiute of Walker Lake, Nevada, who during a solar eclipse had fallen into a deep trance. After he awoke he told of a divine revelation. He had spoken with God, and God had shown him the world of the dead, a pleasant land, full of game, where people were happy and forever young. God told Wovoka to tell his people that they must love one another, live in peace with the whites, and that if they followed these and other instructions they would be reunited with their friends and relatives in a world where there would be no sickness or death. Wovoka was then given a dance to be performed at intervals for five consecutive days. Its performance would hasten the millenium and make the performers happy.

The message of the messiah spread to other tribes, changing and growing as it spread, but generally promising a cataclysmic disaster for whites, a return to the old days, and a reunion with the dead. Once the Ghost Dance crossed the Rockies to the plains, it spread like wildfire and was quickly embraced by the tribes of the southern plains. Cheyenne and Arapaho delegations visited Wovoka and brought back the dance, and the Wichitas were taught the dance by an Arapaho. Throughout the summer of 1891, the Wichitas were preoccupied with dancing, neglecting their crops and stock, to the irritation of their agent. What he failed to realize was that the religion provided the Wichitas with a renewed faith in their future, an ingredient as vital to their crops as seed, and essential to their survival as a distinct people.

84

That the millenium would not arrive was not important. By the summer of 1892, infatuation with the Ghost Dance had declined, and in the following years, when the millenium failed to arrive, it enlisted fewer and fewer followers. Nonetheless, as late as 1917, the agent at Anadarko was still complaining that the Indians had been dancing for twenty-five years.

Allotment of the reservation meant not only a drastic reduction in land holdings, but it also furthered breakdown of the old collective, cooperative nature of Wichita society, in that individuals were forced to scatter out to their widely dispersed allotments in an attempt to eke out a living from the land. It was only a part of the assault made on virtually every aspect of Wichita culture through the first three decades of the twentieth century to make them over into small-scale farmers and stock raisers, little or no different than their white neighbors.

The point of the attack was the government agent who could enforce his wishes by withholding annuity money or by bestowing various kinds of favors, from approving land leases to building houses. Most of the agents appear to have been hard working, and they achieved many laudable things, measured by any standards, such as improved health care and sanitation. They were dedicated, however, to eradicating the old native culture, and they and the bureaucracy of which they were a part also soon had a stake in the continuing dependency of the Wichitas. Thus, the appearance of leaders, supported by vari-

85

WICHITA PEOPLE engaged in a Ghost Dance ceremonial, sometime during the 1890's. The

photographer and date are not recorded in the Bureau of American Ethnology archives.

ous tribal factions, was discouraged, if not prevented, for such men were usually dissidents who challenged or might challenge the policies and actions of the agent and the government.

A different kind of influence was represented by the schooling to which the Wichita children were exposed. They attended a variety of schools, from boarding schools and day schools to missionary and public schools. Agency schools stressed homemaking and agricultural arts, and agents frequently complained that they were unable to give their students as much training in industrial arts as was desirable. Boarding schools had the least satisfactory results, from the point of view of agents, in that the returning graduates often were not equipped to take up the only kind of life that was open to them. In a more subtle sense, in whatever school a Wichita pupil found himself, his education was not directed at equipping him, as a Wichita, with the skills and information necessary to understand and function in or on the margins of a white world. The goal, instead, was to convert him into an indistinguishable part of that world.

In 1900, ninety percent of the Wichitas were still living in grass lodges; by 1931, two grass lodges survived, and these were maintained as nostalgic reminders of the past, but were not used as residences. The shift from grass lodge to American-style frame house is indicative of the changes in Wichita life during this period. Still the Wichitas did not disappear as a distinct tribal culture; they had sur-

A WICHITA VILLAGE of grass-thatched lodges and log cabins near Anadarko, Indian Territory, apparently photographed in the 1890's, documenting the gradual transition from centuries-old tribal housing to Anglo-American rural homes.

GROUP OF WICHITA MEN AND WOMEN photographed at the Omaha Exposition in 1898 by F. A. Rinehart for the Bureau of American Ethnology, showing Wichita adoption of ready-to-wear clothing.

vived many calamities in the past by changing and adapting to new circumstances, and they weathered the aftermath of allotment in much the same way. The very fact that the entire fabric of their life style was under attack inevitably made them react against it, and hold more dear what they considered their own. Part of the appeal of the Ghost Dance was, of course, of this sort, and when its prophecies were not fulfilled, many of its followers embraced a new religious cult, Peyotism.

Like the Ghost Dance, Peyotism was and is an inter-tribal phenomenon, drawing together in belief and practice a multitude of Indian tribes. Unlike the Ghost Dance, Peyotism seeks accommodation with the white world, yet at the same time inspires spiritual and emotional independence from it. Old Man Horse, a Kiowa, is usually credited with introducing the Wichitas to the modern peyote ritual in about 1902, although some Wichitas may have been acquainted with it a few years earlier. It is also said that Wichita medicine men and women long had been acquainted with and used the small, spineless cactus, and in fact, one of the four objects in a medicine bundle employed in a rain ceremony, was a peyote button. In a broader sense, the new cult fitted in with the old belief that spiritual knowledge was acquired directly and personally through revelations, inasmuch as eating peyote induces vivid and colorful visions, often including supernatural beings.

While Peyotism, incorporated as the Native American Church, enlisted many Wichitas, others

90

Courtesy Smithsonian Institution, Bureau of American Ethnology

DANCE LEADERS holding maize and pipe given them at the beginning of the world, photographed by James Mooney in 1892 or 1893. This view bears witness to the fusion of traditional and Christian doctrines in the religious movement at the end of the 19th century.

became members of Christian churches, and for many years the Wichitas were split into two factions according to their religious persuasion.

Until the Wichitas settled on their reservation, no serious attempts had been made to convert them to any branch of Christianity. Then with reservation life came missionaries of a number of faiths, who worked closely, though unofficially, with the government agents. Because none of the old Wichita religious practices was physically harmful, agents had no excuse to ban them. Inasmuch as peyote was not harmful or addictive, its use could not be banned either. Agents could, on the other hand, discourage and often prevent participation in religious or social ceremonies that took people away from home for periods of time ranging up to several weeks. Participation in the Ghost Dance and trekking to various pow-wows and stomp dances were thus abridged by authorities. Peyote meetings, in contrast, lasted a relatively short time, and could be held clandestinely.

THE PRESENT

The Wheeler-Howard or Indian Reorganization Act of 1934 marks the beginning of the modern era for the Wichita people, as well as for other Indians, in the sense that since its passage governmental policy, haltingly, has turned away from the old repressive policies, including coercive assimilation. The act established a policy aimed at expanding and developing Indian lands and resources, it established

92

a revolving credit fund, waived restrictions for Indians seeking civil service jobs, and, among other things, established provisions for tribal organization and incorporation. Oklahoma was excluded from the 1934 act, but the following year Congress passed the Oklahoma Indian Welfare Act, and Oklahoma tribes came under many of the provisions of the earlier legislation. Then the Wichitas established their present tribal organization, composed of a chairman, vice-chairman, treasurer, secretary, and three other members, elected for four-year terms of office. By 1976, the tribe could count about 800 enrolled members, approximately 500 of whom are residents of Caddo County, or the immediate vicinity.

The Wichita tribe has been fortunate in its choice of leaders, and despite slight tribal assets, a number of projects and programs have been initiated which promise to make the Wichita people more secure socially and economically. Among other projects the tribe in 1974 built a 30,000 square-foot office building, which it has leased to the Bureau of Indian Affairs. It has joined with the Caddo and Delaware tribes as the WCD Enterprises, Incorporated, to undertake light industrial and other ventures, and a number of buildings have been completed in an industrial park. The tribe has also been able to benefit from various government programs, obtaining a subsidy from the Department of Agriculture to improve the nutrition of low income families, and other funds have been provided for a water system.

When the government's old Riverside Indian Boarding School was closed in the 1950's, its 2,500 acres reverted to the three affiliated tribes. Ten acres of this land were set aside for the Wichita tribe, and through revenue sharing and donations a community building, dance pavilion, and picnic and camping areas have been constructed. This provides a central, and as it turns out, highly popular meeting place for members of the tribe. An annual dance, generally held in the third week of August, is well on its way to becoming a tradition. The tribal leadership has also begun a number of programs aimed at preserving the tribal heritage and identity. Included in a cultural program, for example, is a project to record tribal songs, and meetings are held in which Wichitas get together to maintain their proficiency in speaking Wichita.

In August, 1946, Congress passed the Indian Claims Commission Act which allowed Indian tribes to file whatever claims they might have against the government. Many years earlier, in 1924, Congress passed an act allowing the Wichitas to bring suit against the government. They did so in an attempt to obtain compensation for lands wrongfully taken from them in Texas, and in Oklahoma west of the Cross Timbers between the Canadian and Red Rivers. The Court of Claims finally rendered a decision in November, 1939, that it did not have the jurisdiction to pass on the aboriginal title to the lands in question, but implied that the Wichita claims to it were not sustained by the evidence. As a conse-

94

Photographs Courtesy of Newton Lamar

MARSHA LAMAR, left, and REGINA LAMAR, right, daughters of President Newton Lamar, wearing contemporary Wichita costumes for dancing.

quence, C. J. Kappler, the attorney of record for the Wichitas, withdrew from the case before the Wichitas could appeal the decision, and an appeal was never made.

As a result of this decision, attorneys viewed any claims case the Wichitas might bring under the Indian Claims Commission Act, to be a poor gamble. Thus, Frank Miller, the Chairman of the tribe during this period, was unable to obtain legal counsel for the tribe in order to file a claim. Finally, in 1968, Omer Luellen of Hinton, Oklahoma, became attorney for the Wichita Tribe, and the tribe was able to enter the Kiowa, Comanche, and Apache, and the Caddo claims cases as an intervenor. Both cases were ultimately thrown out by the Court of Claims, so, as of 1976, the Wichitas had not received compensation for any of the lands they once occupied save those they were forced to part with at the time of allotment.

THE FUTURE

Prophecies of social scientists are often about as trustworthy as the behavior of a Jersey bull, and the few observations made here should be taken with this stricture firmly in mind. Yet it also should be remembered that nations and tribes are continuums, their todays foreshadowed by their yesterdays, their tomorrows but lengthened shadows of the present. From this perspective the future of the Wichita people is seen as bright. For the Wichitas are survivors, persisting through the buffetings of more

96

than four centuries of turmoil and trouble, disaster and defeat. There is good reason to believe, then, that the Wichitas will persist, changing, adapting, absorbing new things, but persevering. Such a forecast probably would have seemed silly in the early decades of this century, for then they numbered only a few hundred people, beleaguered on every side, and their disappearance must have seemed inevitable. Yet a corner was turned in those years and a new and more promising era began.

The future of the Wichita people is also, obviously, bound to the directions the country as a whole takes. From this vantage point the future of the Wichitas is also promising, for it seems extremely unlikely that the government, the American people, or the more aware and politically effective Indian people will ever again permit the adoption of coercive and repressive policies aimed at total assimilation and cultural obliteration. This assertion is based, not so much on a hope that the nation has in its maturity gained wisdom, but on the fact the Wichitas are not so different from other Americans that they are perceived as somehow constituting a threat to them.

A cynic might add that a greedy world has already abstracted from the Wichitas that which is deemed valuable, and that it is unlikely to return to feast on the scraps. A more realistic view would have it that the Wichitas are now competent to fend for themselves in the jungle. No doubt renewed attempts will be made to terminate the special relationships that exist between the Wichitas and the government, and perhaps the long and frustrating struggle to obtain compensation for the lands taken from them will end in failure. Even should these and other unfortunate and unjust things come to pass, the Wichitas now have the organization, and in their elected leaders, possess the knowledge to cope with whatever problems or defeats come their way, and consequently, to prosper. Prosper is used primarily in a commercial, material sense. Sparked by a variety of government programs, the tribe shows promise of flourishing as a business enterprise. This should come as no surprise; the Wichita heritage as traders and businessmen is a long one.

How well and in what ways other aspects of Wichita culture and society will survive, and the forces that will contribute to demise or survival, are much more difficult to foresee. Undoubtedly Wichitas will continue to leave the old reservation lands, perhaps in increasing numbers. Many of them will inexorably be swallowed up ethnically and culturally in mainstream America. Almost surely, others who will disappear as Wichitas will continue to regard themselves, and be regarded by others, as Indians. The number of intertribal marriages that have occurred; the participation in social and religious activities, from powwows to Peyotism, that are Indian rather than Wichita; and the increasing amount of communication and cooperation of all kinds with other Indians, suggest that the transformation from Wichita to detribalized Indian will increase in the years ahead.

98

Photographs Courtesy of Wichita Tribe

GRASSHOUSE, (above) under construction at the Wichita Tribal Park.

GROUP OF DANCERS, (below) at a Wichita Pow-wow.

The Wichitas can be counted on to survive, though probably unable to talk with one another in the old tongue, perhaps forgetful of Bright Shining Woman, and with but a hazy memory of many of the old ways. At the very least, they will have pride in their special heritage, to which it is hoped this volume in a small way has contributed.

SUGGESTED READING

Literature dealing with the history and culture of the Wichita people is fairly extensive, but it is scattered and much of it is in obscure or technical journals. The following list of publications should be available in major libraries.

CURTIS, EDWARD S. The Wichita, pp. 35-104, in *The North American Indian*, vol. 19. Norwood, Mass.: The Plimpton Press, 1930.

A general summary of Wichita culture, and an excellent discussion of ceremonial life.

DORSEY, GEORGE A. *The Mythology of the Wichita.* Publication 21, The Carnegie Institution of Washington. Washington, 1904.

The basic source for Wichita culture and mythology.

JOHN, ELIZABETH A. H. *Storms Brewed in Other Men's Worlds, The Confrontation of Indians, Spanish, and French in the Southwest, 1540-1795.* College Station: Texas A & M University Press, 1975.

A comprehensive history of the region, including Wichita history.

NEWCOMB, W.W., JR. *The Indians of Texas, From Prehistoric to Modern Times*. Chapter 10. The Wichitas: Nations of the North. Austin: The University of Texas Press, 1961.

Summarizes the history and culture of the Wichitas.

ESSADNA, Chief of the Wichitas, photographed about 1875 by William S. Soule, photographer of Fort Sill.

THE AUTHOR

WILLIAM W. NEWCOMB, JR. is Professor of Anthropology, the University of Texas at Austin, and Director of the Texas Memorial museum. A native of Michigan, he received B.A., M.A., and Ph.D. degrees from the University of Michigan.

Newcomb has conducted ethnographic research among the Delaware Indians of Oklahoma, archeological investigations in Texas and Arkansas, and ethnohistoric research on Apache, Comanche, Wichita, and other Indians. He was a member of a team of anthropologists, supported by the National Science Foundation, that made "A Pilot Study of Wichita Indian Archeology and Ethnohistory," and he has served as a witness for the Wichita Indian Tribe before the Indian Claims Commission.

He is the author of *The Indians of Texas* (1961), *The Rock Art of Texas Indians* (1967), and various articles and chapters in a number of publications. His most recent book (1974) is *North American Indians: An Anthropological Perspective*.

104